DIFFERENTIAL DIAGNOSIS OF APHASIA
WITH THE MINNESOTA TEST

Second Edition, Revised

Differential Diagnosis of Aphasia
with the Minnesota Test

Hildred Schuell, Ph.D.

Revised by Joyce W. Sefer, M.A.

UNIVERSITY OF MINNESOTA PRESS, Minneapolis

Preface to Revised Edition

This revised edition was prepared to take account of major changes made in the Schuell classification system of aphasic patients and to add data for two of the diagnostic groups.

During the years between the publication of the Minnesota Test in 1965 and Hildred Schuell's death in 1970, she had come to the conclusion that the syndromes she had originally labeled "minor" were not minor at all, but only seemed so as a function of the population under study. Data from a collaborative study on a Japanese population supported this contention (Hildred Schuell and Kazuhisa Nagai, "Aphasia Studies," in *Geriatrics*, October-November 1969). Therefore the original classification into five major and two minor syndromes needed to be changed. She started to cluster the seven syndromes into three "mild," one "moderate," and three "severe" categories. After her death, when it fell to James J. Jenkins, Robert Shaw, and me to revise her *Aphasia in Adults* (first published in 1964; revised edition to be issued in 1973), we did not pursue this approach because we became convinced that such a classification would encourage even trained clinicians to use the mean number of errors of a given patient *diagnostically*, which would lead to many misdiagnoses. In revising the classification system we decided against renumbering the categories to place the two groupings previously called minor in logical sequence, since this would inevitably have led to confusion among users of the test. Instead the numerical labels were dropped and the descriptive terms were adopted. In addition we decided that the term *persisting dysarthria* (used in conjunction with Minor Category B) was not specific enough, and the syndrome was renamed *persisting dysfluency*, which more precisely describes the dysfluencies of these patients that resemble primary stuttering. The syndrome nomenclature used in this revision of *Differential Diagnosis of Aphasia*, as well as in *Schuell's Aphasia in Adults*, is as follows, arranged in order of increasing severity for the groupings as a whole: simple aphasia (formerly Group 1); aphasia with visual involvement (formerly Group 2); mild aphasia with persisting dysfluency (formerly Minor Category B); aphasia with scattered findings compatible with generalized brain damage (formerly Group 4); aphasia with sensorimotor involvement (formerly Group 3); aphasia with intermittent imperception (formerly Minor Category A; abbreviated "auditory"); and irreversible aphasia.

Dr. Schuell had collected new data on the published version of the test from patients at the Minneapolis Veterans Administration Hospital, where she was director of the Aphasia Section, and these have been analyzed by diagnostic category. Unfortunately it was not possible, after her death, to locate the original raw data on which the means and percentages reported in the first edition of *Differential Diagnosis of Aphasia* were based; consequently, for the revised edition the data gathered on the published version of the test could not be combined with the earlier data. The means and percentages for the original data in each of the categories as reported in the first edition have been retained here because the later data reflect the scores of a smaller number of patients and because the results were remarkably similar for the two sets of data. However, the means and percentages calculated for the new data from patients in the former "minor" categories, persisting dysfluency and auditory, have been added to the tabulations of this revised edition. (The first edition did not include statistics on persisting dysfluency; statistics as given in the first edition for the auditory group are here labeled "auditory (1)," with the new data labeled "auditory (2).")

Preface to Revised Edition

It was my privilege to work with Hildred Schuell at the Minneapolis VA Hospital and to discuss with her the proposed changes in the classification system. I hope that these changes, and the supplementary data, will add to the clarity and utility of the Minnesota Test. Preparation of this revised edition of *Differential Diagnosis of Aphasia with the Minnesota Test* was supported in part by grants to the University of Minnesota, Center for Research in Human Learning, from the National Science Foundation, GB 17590, and the National Institute of Child Health and Human Development, HD-01136.

Joyce W. Sefer
Center for Research in Human Learning
Minneapolis, Minnesota
August 1972

Table of Contents

DIFFERENTIAL DIAGNOSIS OF APHASIA
WITH THE MINNESOTA TEST

1

Interpreting Test Results

The Minnesota Test for Differential Diagnosis of Aphasia was designed to permit the examiner to observe the level at which language performance breaks down in each of the principal language modalities, since this is essentially what there is to observe in aphasia. A sensitive test, however, should do more than indicate performance levels. Tests can be constructed that reveal critical dimensions of impairment within specific modalities, and this the Minnesota Test has attempted to do. In other words, the Minnesota Test looks at the language behavior of aphasic patients, and then proceeds to ask questions about the nature of the disruptions that occur.

After some general discussion of differential diagnosis of aphasia, this chapter will be concerned with recurring patterns of impairment identified on the Minnesota Test, with the prognosis for recovery from aphasia for patients in each of the defined categories, and with the correlations between the principal diagnostic categories and findings obtained on neurological examinations. A brief review of the development of the Minnesota Test concludes the chapter.

The remainder of the monograph considers the Minnesota Test section by section, discussing the nature and the purpose of each part of the examination and describing individual tests in terms of the kinds of observations permitted, error distributions obtained from

3

aphasic and nonaphasic subjects, and, in most cases, factorial structure and correlations with other tests.

THE NATURE OF APHASIC IMPAIRMENT

It seems meaningful to define aphasia as a reduction of available language that crosses all language modalities and may or may not be complicated by perceptual or sensorimotor involvement, by various forms of dysarthria, or by other sequelae of brain damage. The overall pattern of involvement varies from patient to patient, and this variation makes differential diagnosis possible.

Some aphasic patients show reduction of language and nothing more. In the classification system to be described below, this pattern is labeled simple aphasia. Patients with simple aphasia find it harder to understand what they hear and what they read than they used to. They have trouble finding words and expressing ideas in speech and in writing. They make verbal errors, but these tend to be the same kinds of errors other people make under conditions of fatigue or inattention, or with partial loss of a once familiar language through disuse.

There is nothing bizarre about aphasic language behavior. The difference between aphasic and nonaphasic disruptions of language is chiefly one of degree. All of us occasionally misread and mishear and misinterpret what we read and what we hear. None of us has perfect recall of the verbal stimuli to which we attend. Highly trained professional speakers garble words sometimes. All of us absently say the wrong word once in a while, and find occasion to ask, "Did I say Tuesday? I meant Wednesday," or words to this effect. All of us sometimes have trouble finding the precise word we are searching for, and all of us have been embarrassed by inability to recall a name we should know. It has been pointed out that utterances recalled from dreams have some of the characteristics of aphasic language. All these observations suggest that language behavior follows general laws in aphasia as in other circumstances.

The reduction of language in aphasia may be mild or severe or somewhere in between. In addition it may be complicated by involvement of other systems that contribute to language behavior. In some patients cerebral involvement of visual processes may produce further interference with reading or writing. In others impairment of the sensorimotor system may disrupt both perception and production of phonemes or production alone. Still others may show weakness of the speech musculature and present aphasia with dysarthria.

Probably all aphasic patients show some impairment of auditory processes, because language, learned by ear, remains dependent upon discrimination, recognition, and recall of learned auditory patterns, and upon auditory feedback processes. Some aphasic patients, however, tend to behave as though they were deaf, even when pure tone audiometry indicates normal thresholds for sound. In the older literature this condition was labeled pure word deafness, or auditory verbal agnosia. Penfield and Roberts [5] preferred the term *partial auditory imperception,* observing that patients with this disorder always recognized some words under some conditions. Ability to perceive spoken language tends to increase gradually with time. The term *intermittent auditory imperception* is used here, since this describes the phenomenon better.

It is meaningful to talk about simple aphasia when there is reduction of available language and nothing more. It is also meaningful to talk about aphasia with visual involvement, aphasia with sensorimotor involvement, aphasia with dysfluency, and aphasia with intermittent auditory imperception, as well as about other patterns that can be demonstrated in a clinical population.

THE SIGNIFICANCE OF DIFFERENTIAL DIAGNOSIS

Differential diagnosis is the basis of both description and prediction in aphasia.

Careful description of aphasic impairment provides a guide for treatment, since therapy must deal with the disabilities that are present. It must be concerned with the level at which disruption occurs in each language modality, and with the processes underlying observed disruptions. Defective articulation, for example, may reflect weakness of the speech musculature, sensorimotor impairment, or imperfect retrieval of learned auditory patterns. Whether the clinician decides to work with the musculature or to work through the ear depends upon accurate diagnosis, and choice of method will have an effect on progress.

Predicting the course of the disorder is important in relation to long-term planning for the aphasic patient. Jenkins et al. [4] found a correspondence between patterns of aphasic impairment revealed by testing and neurological deficit. In other words, patterns of aphasic impairment reflect loci and extent of brain damage, and consequently are related to recovery of function. As a result well-studied patterns of aphasic deficit should be expected to carry reliable prognoses for recovery of language functions, and they do. The general compatibility of neurological findings is chiefly verifying information, however, for language is one of the highest and most complex of cerebral functions. Consequently when language deficit is present it is one of the most sensitive indicators of brain damage that we have.

LIMITS OF PREDICTION

It is not possible to predict the course and outcome of aphasia unless the patient is neurologically stable. No one can predict which symptoms will persist and which will subside during the acute period that follows cerebral trauma. Healing takes place in the brain. Swelling goes down, bleeding is absorbed, and some degree of collateral circulation may be established. Hence, symptoms that reflected temporary reduction of function in one or another part of the brain may disappear.

The consensus is that most of the spontaneous recovery in aphasia occurs during the first three months. This is an arbitrary limit, and exceptions occur in both directions, but most investigators agree that significant changes do not often occur of themselves after this period and that one cannot be sure of obtaining a reliable test much earlier. Patients can of course be tested whenever they are alert enough to cooperate in testing, and treatment can be initiated. During the early stages, however, the clinician cannot safely predict the course of the disorder on the basis of the obtained test, and must be ready to adapt methods and materials from day to day to keep up with functional changes as they occur. After patients are neurologically stable, performance is consistent and prediction tends to be highly reliable.

Differential diagnosis is not possible on the basis of quantitative scoring of tests alone, because patients may fail the same tests for different reasons. On a test such as naming objects, for example, one patient may call a chair a table because he has difficulty finding words, while another may respond *te,* because he cannot make a *ch* or an *r* sound. One patient may make errors in writing sentences to dictation because the words are meaningless to him. Another may understand the words but cannot retain the sentence because his verbal retention span is inadequate. A third patient may not remember what an *x* or a *j* looks like, confuse *m*'s and *w*'s, and write *nit* for *night* and *grenn* for *green* because he cannot remember the visual forms of these words. Still another patient may write *red* for *green* and *dark* for *night.*

This means that it is necessary to ask not only how many but what kind of errors a patient made on a given task. It is possible to describe patterns of aphasic impairment in terms of test profiles that reflect quantitative errors, but it is more meaningful to describe the performance of an individual patient in terms of the kinds of errors he makes, or clinical signs.

The importance of clinical signs is clear when we reflect that not only involvement of the language system itself but involvement of any of the contributing systems may be at any level from mild to severe. While this factor results in a wide range of variability within diagnostic categories, it also contributes to their stability. Since diagnostic categories are determined by pattern of impairment rather than severity of involvement, classification remains constant through all stages of recovery, as test-retest profiles show [4]. The over-all pattern of aphasic impairment is a better predictor than age, educational or occupational level, extent of neurological involvement, or initial severity of aphasia [4].

Standard test scores are meaningless when dealing with aphasic populations which are heterogeneous in age, intelligence, cultural milieu, medical history, locus and extent of brain damage, and severity and duration of aphasia. The most important reason, however,

7

for rejecting standard scores is that they yield no information about the *nature of interference* with performance on individual tests or about the *over-all pattern of impairment,* which are the two most significant variables in aphasia. It follows that the most effective way of interpreting test data is in terms of clinical signs and total test pattern.

CATEGORIES OF APHASIA

The pages that follow provide a description of the seven major categories of aphasia that were identified by analysis of data gathered in use of the Minnesota Test over a period of years, with definition, relevant clinical signs, a list of the most differentiating tests, and prognosis for recovery. (See Jenkins et al. [4] for more extended discussion and data.)

Simple Aphasia

Definition

Simple aphasia is defined as reduction of available language in all modalities with no specific perceptual or sensorimotor impairment and no dysarthria.

Signs

1. Vocabulary is reduced in all language modalities. Word-finding difficulty may be obvious, or the patient may only report that he cannot remember names as well as he used to.

2. Errors in recognizing words and producing words in responses increase when less common words are used or required.

3. The most common word-finding error is confusion between words related in meaning or experience, such as *table* and *chair, man* and *woman, Monday* and *Tuesday, June* and *July,* and *red* and *green.*

4. Inconsistent mispronunciations sometimes occur. These mispronunciations are not related to articulation difficulty, can be corrected readily by ear, and gradually disappear as language increases.

5. Verbal retention span is reduced in all modalities. Errors increase as verbal stimuli or required responses increase in length.

6. Speech sometimes sounds confused because the patient forgets

what he was asked, what he started to say, or what he has just said. He may follow some random association and lose the original intent.

7. The patient makes the same kind of errors in finding words and producing sentences in writing as he makes in speech.

8. The patient frequently loses the meaning of what he reads because he cannot remember the content of preceding sentences or paragraphs.

9. Some functional language is retained in all modalities.

10. In general, speech and writing, which require the patient to produce verbal sequences, show more impairment than auditory comprehension or reading, where verbal patterns are supplied.

Most Discriminating Tests

1. Auditory tests: understanding sentences, understanding a paragraph, repeating digits, repeating sentences.

2. Reading tests: understanding sentences and a paragraph.

3. Speech and language tests: defining words, describing a picture, retelling a paragraph.

4. Writing: producing written sentences, writing sentences to dictation, writing a paragraph.

Prognosis

Excellent recovery of all language skills. Treatment is usually required for maximal return of language and successful vocational adjustment.

Aphasia with Visual Involvement

Definition

Aphasia with visual involvement is characterized by reduction of available language in all modalities, with coexisting impairment of discrimination, recognition, and recall of learned visual symbols.

Signs

1. All signs reported for simple aphasia.

2. Reading and writing show more impairment than auditory comprehension or speech.

9

Differential Diagnosis of Aphasia

3. There is consistent impairment of visual discrimination, and of recognition and recall of learned visual patterns. This may be shown by any or all of the following signs, depending upon severity of visual involvement.

4. Patients tend to confuse letters with similar visual configurations on matching, pointing to letters named by the examiner, and writing letters dictated in random order. Letters most commonly confused are *E F, W M, A H N Z K, C G, O Q,* and *P B R* in upper-case print; *p b d q, t f, h n u r, w m,* and *m n* in lower-case print, and *b f, h k, h y, y j, u w, m n,* and *a o* in script.

5. Distortions of letter forms appear on copying and writing.

6. Horizontal and vertical reversals of letters occur.

7. There is a tendency toward phonetic spelling and special difficulty with silent letters and double letters in words.

8. Patients misread and miswrite words with similar visual configurations, such as *store* and *stone, watch* and *match, dark* and *park, house* and *horse.*

9. Patients frequently read the first part of the word correctly and guess the end.

10. Oral spelling tends to be better than written spelling. The patient may frequently spell a word aloud correctly and write it incorrectly because of impaired recall of letter forms.

11. The patient may use kinesthetic and proprioceptive cues to aid defective visual recognition or recall. He may sometimes be observed to trace a letter on the page or in the air before naming or writing it.

12. With severe visual impairment, matching, copying, and drawing may be defective, and the patient may be unable to recognize or to produce any letter forms.

Most Discriminating Tests

1. Visual and reading tests: matching forms, matching letters, matching words to pictures, oral reading.

2. Visuomotor and writing tests: drawing, copying, writing letters to dictation, written and oral spelling, producing sentences spontaneously, writing sentences to dictation, writing a paragraph.

Prognosis

Excellent recovery of language, as in simple aphasia. Reading and writing improve more slowly than speech. Rate of performance tends to remain retarded, and occasional inconsistent visual errors tend to persist. Former reading and writing levels are approximated, however.

Mild Aphasia with Persisting Dysfluency

Definition

This syndrome resembles simple aphasia, except for the accompaniment of persisting dysfluency.

Signs

1. All the signs reported for simple aphasia.
2. Consistent articulatory errors.
3. Speech is slow and nonfluent.
4. Articulation disintegrates when less common or longer words are required.
5. Articulation disintegrates as longer responses are attempted.
6. Articulation disintegrates whenever the patient attempts to talk faster.
7. Connected speech disintegrates when the patient does not exert conscious control.

Most Discriminating Tests

1. Auditory tests: repeating digits, repeating sentences.
2. Visual and reading tests: oral reading.
3. Speech and language tests: imitation of gross movements, repeating monosyllables, repeating phrases, all tests requiring verbal responses.
4. Visuomotor and writing tests: producing written sentences, writing sentences to dictation, writing a paragraph.

Prognosis

Excellent recovery of language, as in simple aphasia. Normal articulation patterns can be acquired, but disintegrate when conscious control is not exerted. Automaticity and fluency are not regained. It

Differential Diagnosis of Aphasia

should be noted that dysfluency may occur in the presence or the absence of aphasia, defined as a reduction of available language.

Aphasia with Scattered Findings Compatible with Generalized Brain Damage

Definition

This grouping is characterized by reduction of available language, with scattered findings that usually include both visual involvement and some degree of dysarthria. The patient is able to communicate voluntarily in either speech or writing, though both processes are usually defective to some extent.

Signs

1. There is reduction of vocabulary and of verbal retention span.

2. Visual impairment may be mild, consisting only of blurring of fine discriminations in reading and writing.

3. Visual impairment may be severe, and characterized by intermittent blurring and obfuscation.

4. In addition to the visual signs reported for aphasia with visual involvement, the patient may have difficulty following a line of print and keeping his place in reading.

5. Spatial perception and directionality may be impaired.

6. There may be mild dysarthria characterized by general slurring of speech.

7. There may be severe dysarthria resulting from paralysis of the tongue, the soft palate, the pharynx, and occasionally of a vocal cord. These symptoms are usually accompanied by difficulty in swallowing. Sometimes the tongue or the soft palate alone may be involved.

8. There may be persisting emotional lability.

9. There is some functional communication in either speech or writing or both.

Most Discriminating Tests

1. Auditory tests: understanding sentences and a paragraph.

2. Visual and reading tests: matching tests, understanding sentences and a paragraph, oral reading.

12

Interpreting Test Results

3. Speech and language tests: gross movements of the speech musculature, repeating phrases, retelling a paragraph.

4. Visuomotor and writing tests: drawing and copying tests, object assembly tests (Wechsler or Binet), producing written sentences, writing sentences to dictation, writing a paragraph.

Prognosis

Limited by the general neurophysiological status of the patient. Patients with scattered findings often work well with the clinician, and make gains in auditory comprehension, word finding, and intelligibility. They are usually incapable of persistent self-directed effort.

Aphasia with Sensorimotor Involvement

Definition

Aphasia with sensorimotor involvement is characterized by severe reduction of language in all modalities accompanied by difficulty in discriminating, producing, and sequencing phonemes.

Signs

1. Auditory comprehension is good for common words and short language units, but verbal retention span is severely impaired. It may be reduced to three or four words of connected speech and two or three digits.

2. Phoneme discrimination is poor. The patient may hear no differences between short vowels. He tends to confuse letters whose names sound alike, such as *b c d e g p t, i y, h j k,* and sounds with similar loci and patterns of articulation, such as *p b m, t d n l, f v,* and *k g.*

3. Patients can usually match common words to pictures. Visual recognition of printed words usually exceeds auditory recognition of the same words.

4. Reading comprehension tends to break down at the level of simple sentences.

5. Sensorimotor patients usually have difficulty in producing rapid alternating movements of the speech musculature.

6. Repetition is defective, and characterized by omission, distortion, and substitution of phonemes.

13

Differential Diagnosis of Aphasia

7. Emission of speech is slow and labored.

8. Articulatory errors increase as more complex motor patterns or longer verbal sequences are required, although articulation of frequently used words and phrases becomes normal.

9. Voice quality is normal, although the patient may be unable to imitate phonation voluntarily on first attempts.

10. Vocabulary is usually reduced to a few common words or phrases, or the patient may have no speech on initial examination.

11. As language is recovered, patients tend to communicate in single words or short phrases. When patients first attempt to combine words, sentences tend to be telegraphic. This is also true of children when they are learning to talk, and only limited language is available [3].

12. Copying and drawing are usually intact, but writing is limited by the severe reduction of language.

Most Discriminating Tests

1. Auditory tests: identifying items named serially, pointing to letters named in random order, following directions.

2. Visual and reading tests: matching words to pictures, matching printed to spoken words, understanding sentences.

3. Speech and language tests: rapid alternating movements, repeating monosyllables, naming pictures, producing sentences.

4. Writing tests: writing letters dictated in random order, written spelling, producing written sentences, and writing sentences to dictation.

Prognosis

Recovery of limited but functional language skills. Patients are able to communicate needs through intelligible speech, although responses are often slow and labored and reflect severe disruption of language processes. Reading and writing remain limited, also.

Aphasia with Intermittent Auditory Imperception

Definition

Aphasia with intermittent auditory imperception is characterized by severe impairment of auditory perception, with some functional speech usually retained or recovered early.

14

Signs
1. Patients frequently behave as though they did not hear.
2. Patients make errors in pointing to common objects. Recognition tends to be an all or none process. The patient usually either points promptly and correctly or appears confused and bewildered.
3. Patients make errors in following simple directions.
4. Patients sometimes respond better to long than to short auditory stimuli, probably because of the redundancy of language. In these cases they are responding to occasional words they perceive, which furnish clues that enable them to make occasional successful guesses.
5. Patients usually make errors in matching common words to pictures. They are unable to read aloud initially and usually have little more than chance success on sentence comprehension. They tend to utilize visual cues with increasing effectiveness, however.
6. They usually cannot repeat, although this improves with practice. Initial attempts may produce jargon.
7. Some spontaneous speech that sounds normal is usually present or emerges early.
8. Although the patient has a high verbal output, he usually has difficulty in naming objects and producing specific responses. Language tends to be vague and general.
9. Writing is usually limited, since patients have difficulty in perceiving sequences and recalling names of letters. They may learn to write a list of words in sequence but be completely baffled if the same words are dictated in a different order.

Most Discriminating Tests
1. Auditory tests: recognizing common objects named by the examiner, discriminating between paired words, following directions, repeating digits, repeating sentences.
2. Reading tests: matching words to pictures, matching printed to spoken words, understanding sentences, oral reading.
3. Speech and language tests: repeating monosyllables, naming pictures.

15

Differential Diagnosis of Aphasia

4. Visuomotor and writing tests: writing letters to dictation, written spelling, producing written sentences.

Prognosis

Limited but functional recovery. Auditory comprehension usually improves to a functionally significant degree, although residual difficulty tends to persist and to be reflected in all language modalities.

Irreversible Aphasic Syndrome

Definition

The irreversible aphasic syndrome is characterized by almost complete loss of functional language skills in all modalities.

Signs

1. The patient makes errors in pointing to common objects named by the examiner. He usually scores below the first percentile for adults on the Ammons *Full-Range Picture Vocabulary Test.*

2. The patient makes errors in following simple directions.

3. The patient may be able to match some common words to pictures. He cannot read aloud, and has no more than chance success on tests for sentence comprehension.

4. Some reactive speech may occur, but the patient cannot name objects, or give simple biographical information.

5. He is unable to write a list of common words or simple sentences spontaneously or to dictation. Although some patients are able to copy, they have no functional writing.

Most Discriminating Tests

1. Auditory tests: recognizing common objects named by the examiner, identifying items named serially, following directions.

2. Visual and reading tests: matching words to pictures, understanding sentences.

3. Speech and language tests: imitating gross movements, counting to 20, naming pictures, giving biographical information.

4. Visuomotor and writing tests: writing letters dictated in random order, written spelling.

Prognosis

Auditory comprehension may show functional improvement, and reactive responses increase, but language does not become functional or voluntary in any modality.

NEUROLOGICAL CORRELATES

This section is based on a study of 180 aphasic subjects in the Minneapolis Veterans Hospital reported by Jenkins et al. [4].

In summarizing the data in Tables 1 through 4, it is possible to say that simple aphasia, visual, and persisting dysfluency patients presented a picture of generally mild neurological involvement compatible with limited lesions. They presented relatively few complicating conditions, and tended to make good recovery in all areas of rehabilitation. Visual field defects were more prevalent in visual and auditory patients than in other groups.

Sensorimotor patients presented a picture of severe neurological involvement but with relatively few complicating conditions. They made good progress in rehabilitation in spite of severe limitations. They achieved ambulation with a brace and a cane. They learned to care for their physical needs with one good hand. They achieved functional communication in spite of persisting limitations of language. The findings are compatible with a large lesion in an otherwise intact brain.

Although patients with scattered findings did not show the extensive neurological damage found in sensorimotor patients, the inci-

Table 1. History and Etiology of 180 Patients Studied

Item	Degree of Freedom	Chi Square	Probability
Age (oldest: scattered findings, irreversible)	4	52.5	<.001
Educational level (lowest: scattered findings, irreversible)	8	27.3	<.0005
Incidence CVA's			
Highest: sensorimotor, irreversible	1	4.69	<.05
Lowest: simple, visual, persisting dysfluency	1	4.45	<.05
Complete thrombosis of internal carotid or middle cerebral (highest: sensorimotor, auditory, irreversible)	1	14.45	<.001

Table 2. Indices of Severity of Neurological Involvement for Patients

Neurological Involvement	Degree of Freedom	Chi Square	Probability
Paralysis or paresis of extremities			
Highest: sensorimotor, irreversible	1	23.3	<.001
Lowest: simple, visual, auditory	1	15.5	<.001
Paralysis only			
Highest: sensorimotor, irreversible.....	1	7.84	<.01
Lowest: simple, visual, auditory	1	15.54	<.001
Facial paralysis			
Highest: persisting dysfluency, sensorimotor, irreversible	1	5.44	<.025
Lowest: simple, visual, scattered findings, auditory	1	5.44	<.025
Sensory reduction			
Highest: visual, irreversible	1	4.30	<.05
Lowest: simple, persisting dysfluency, auditory	1	6.70	<.01
Focal EEG findings			
Highest: persisting dysfluency, auditory, irreversible	1	6.11	<.025
Lowest: simple, scattered findings......	1	4.38	<.05

Table 3. Complicating Conditions in Patients

Condition [a]	Degree of Freedom	Chi Square	Probability
Hypertension (highest: scattered findings, irreversible)	1	14.9	<.001
Abnormal EKG (highest: scattered findings, irreversible)	1	15.2	<.001
Previous episodes (highest: scattered findings, irreversible)	1	3.97	<.05
Palatal, laryngeal, pharyngeal weakness (highest: scattered findings, irreversible)..	1	42.5	<.001
Tongue weakness (highest: scattered findings, irreversible)	1	64.7	<.001
Bilateral neurological findings (highest: scattered findings, auditory)	1	28.3	<.001
Visual field defect (highest: visual, auditory)	1	19.6	<.001
Abnormal mental status (highest: scattered findings, irreversible)	1	63.9	<.001

[a] Bilateral weakness of extremities was found only in the scattered-findings patients.

18

Interpreting Test Results

Table 4. Course or Outcome for Patients

Course or Outcome	Degree of Freedom	Chi Square	Probability
Initial self-care evaluation (lowest: scattered findings, irreversible)	1	29.8	<.001
Final self-care evaluation (lowest: scattered findings, irreversible)	1	14.0	<.001
Initial ambulation (lowest: scattered findings, irreversible)	1	21.6	<.001
Final ambulation (lowest: scattered findings, irreversible)	1	11.52	<.001
Vocational training or gainful employment (lowest: scattered findings, irreversible)	1	43.3	<.001
Known deaths, further episodes, or commitment (highest: scattered findings, irreversible)	1	12.4	<.001

dence of many complicating conditions pointed to generalized bilateral damage throughout the brain. While these subjects had more residual function than sensorimotor patients, they were usually unable to integrate their resources and move toward recovery as sensorimotor patients did. Scattered-findings patients had many physiological complaints. They complained of headaches, blurring of vision, tinnitus, dizziness, shortness of breath, fatigue, and pain. They were often more concerned about having another stroke, having a heart attack, or dying than they were about aphasia. This is understandable, and frequently proved to be realistic. Behavioral symptoms in scattered-findings patients varied from mild emotional lability or mild confusion to unremitting organic psychoses. Because of the wide range of concomitant conditions prognosis must be considered in relation to the physiological and psychological condition of the patient, rather than in relation to the severity of aphasia. The scattered pattern of test errors is often symptomatic of alterations that affect more than speech.

Patients with intermittent auditory imperception demonstrated no bilateral weakness of the extremities, but bilateral damage was indicated by the results of neurological testing in a large percentage of these patients. They did not demonstrate the behavior that the scattered-findings group presented. One of the 19 studied had emotional lability which he learned to control early. These patients were

19

hard working and concerned about their inability to use language. They generally made good gains with treatment and achieved functional communication. Most achieved good ambulation and self-care, but because of the severity of aphasia, few were able to find employment.

The investigators had predicted the severe neurological involvement found in irreversible aphasics, but were surprised at the high incidence of complicating conditions found in the study. This was probably a result of clinical impressions being derived from those subjects who were alert and responsive and able to participate in therapy. These patients naturally tended to be the most intact individuals in the group.

The investigators consider that the neurological findings supported the hypothesis that the differences between diagnostic categories were true differences related to loci and extent of lesions and incidence of complicating conditions, as well as to patterns of aphasic impairment revealed by testing.

DEVELOPMENT OF THE MINNESOTA TEST

Form 1 of *The Minnesota Test for Differential Diagnosis of Aphasia* was constructed during the summer of 1948. Principles governing the organization and selection of tests were as follows: (1) The test should explore differences in the behavior of aphasic and nonaphasic subjects in all language modalities, since this is what is observable in aphasia. (2) Tests in each language modality should be graduated in difficulty, in order to permit comparison of successive performances of the same subjects at appropriate time intervals. (3) The test should include a variety of nonlanguage tasks, since there are complex processes underlying language events that cannot be directly observed but must be inferred from relevant kinds of discriminatory behavior. (4) The test should be both comprehensive and detailed, in order to differentiate diverse clinical syndromes resulting from brain damage. In short, a test was desired that would constitute an operational description of aphasia, provide an objective method by which clinicians could evaluate changes that occurred

20

during the course of therapy, and serve as an instrument for longitudinal studies as well.

From the fall of 1949 the test was administered routinely to all patients referred to the Aphasia Section of the Neurology Service of the Minneapolis Veterans Administration Hospital upon admission and discharge, and results were recorded on data sheets. At the same time the staff continued to explore additional tests as they were published and to devise new tests to explore hypotheses suggested by clinical observations. These tests were administered to both aphasic and nonaphasic subjects, and results were tabulated and analyzed. Data obtained from the Minnesota Test were analyzed at approximately yearly intervals, and error distributions studied. The test was then revised as a result of the findings obtained and experience gained from clinical trials.

Between 1949 and 1954 the test underwent five major revisions, and in one form or another was administered to approximately 500 aphasic subjects. In general revisions were of three kinds. Sometimes test instructions or test items were altered to facilitate administration or obtain better patient response. Sometimes tests were deleted because patient responses were equivocal, because tests did not discriminate adequately between aphasic and nonaphasic subjects, were duplicated by other tests (passed or failed by the same subjects), or contributed little to understanding of aphasic disabilities. Eventually most performance tests were eliminated except some used to explore visual and spatial behavior. Finally new tests considered promising on the basis of experimental trials were added to the battery.

By 1958 Form 6 had been administered to 155 aphasic patients on the Aphasia Section of the Neurology Service of the Minneapolis Veterans Administration Hospital who were neurologically stable and showed no evidence of psychosis or regressive behavior [4]. Test-retest results on admission and discharge were available for 73 subjects. Form 6 was also administered to 50 nonaphasic subjects on the medical wards of the same hospital, who approximated the age distribution of the aphasic series. In both groups 38 per cent of the subjects were under fifty years of age, and 62 per cent were over fifty [10]. Aphasic subjects had a slightly higher educational and vocational level than nonaphasic subjects.

Research Grant B 1948, from the Institute of Neurological Diseases and Blindness, continued under Center Grant NB-03364, made possible extensive analysis of the data obtained. Language tests were found to be scalable across modalities [6]. Factor analysis of test data obtained from 157 aphasic subjects yielded five meaningful dimensions: a language factor that crossed all language modalities and rejected nonlanguage tests; a visual factor that included both reading and writing tests; a visuospatial factor; a factor related to gross movements of the speech and pharyngeal musculature; and a factor of stimulus equivalence [10]. Test-retest results were consistent for all diagnostic categories, and aphasic and nonaphasic subjects were clearly separable on the basis of magnitude and distribution of test errors [4].

Correlations between test sections were generally high for aphasic subjects, reflecting over-all language deficit and severity of aphasia. They were low for nonaphasic subjects, reflecting randomness of errors. The highest correlations for nonaphasic subjects were between reading and writing tests. Although these did not approach the correlation coefficients obtained by aphasic subjects, it was considered that they represented a degree of consistency related to educational level. Finally, the categories of aphasia determined by patterns of impairment identified on the Minnesota Test correlated with findings obtained on neurological examinations in a meaningful manner and to a significant degree [4], as described above.

Results were so generally consistent that it was tempting to publish Form 6 with no changes. However, continued experimentation had suggested alterations that promised to make the test a more sensitive instrument and increase the information it yielded. Consequently Form 7 was set up in 1958 and administered to 75 aphasic and 50 nonaphasic subjects, selected according to the previously used criteria.

The Minnesota Test for Differential Diagnosis of Aphasia published in 1965 is Form 8. Except for the addition of three tests used experimentally since 1958, and deletion of tests duplicated by other tests, changes from Forms 6 and 7 are minor. For the most part they consist of deletion of test items missed by a critical number of non-aphasic subjects in older age groups. Because of these changes the number of subjects for whom standardization data are reported in the chapters that follow is smaller than the actual number to whom any test was administered in the long history of test development. It seemed reasonable, however, to prefer refined tests to larger series of subjects.

After publication of the test, collection of test scores continued, with the result that standardized data for two groups have been added to this revised edition of the present volume: 7 patients with persisting dysfluency and 17 with intermittent auditory imperception (the latter group is labeled "auditory (2)" in the tabulations that follow; the subjects with this diagnosis who were tested before publication of the Minnesota Test are labeled "auditory (1)" — see the Preface to Revised Edition for further details about the new data).

In the fifth printing, 1972, of *The Minnesota Test for Differential Diagnosis of Aphasia* a few minor changes were made, primarily in the order of items in two of the tests.

The Minnesota Test consists of five sections: 9 tests for auditory disturbances, 9 tests for visual and reading disturbances, 15 tests for speech and language disturbances, 10 tests for visuomotor and writing disturbances, and 4 tests for disturbances of numerical relations and arithmetic processes. Besides the present volume, test publications include the *Administrative Manual for the Minnesota Test for Differential Diagnosis of Aphasia,* which contains the complete test; the individual test booklets, designed to constitute a clinical record for each patient; and the *Card Materials* (in two packs), designed by Lawrence Benson. All are published by the University of Minnesota Press, Minneapolis [6].

It may be useful to comment on test length. Short tests for aphasia cannot be considered satisfactory. First it is necessary to test various areas of language behavior lest aspects of aphasic deficit be overlooked. Secondly, it is necessary to include analytic tests in each modality, to determine why a subject failed a given task. For example, as already noted, one subject might fail to write words to dictation because the sound patterns he heard had no meaning for him. Another might fail the same test because he could not recall the visual configurations of the letters. These possibilities must be explored by additional tests asking specific questions. This is the process of differential diagnosis.

Finally, there are patients with severe aphasia who can perform only on extremely "easy" tests, and patients with mild aphasia who show impairment only on the "hardest" tests in each section, when "easy" and "hard" are defined by the number of aphasic subjects passing or failing each test. In between are subjects who make no errors on the "easy" tests and cannot perform at all on the "hard" ones. It is therefore necessary to include tests of graduated difficulty in each test section.

The testing process itself can be shortened, however, by obtaining a base line and a ceiling for each subject, since tests in each section are scaled according to difficulty. To obtain a base line, the examiner selects the highest test he thinks the patient can pass in each test section. If the patient makes more than one error he goes back to an easier test, until the criterion of not more than one error is met. The examiner then proceeds with the harder tests in order, until the patient fails approximately 90 per cent of the items on any test, which may be considered the test ceiling. Thus each patient is tested only at the level on which he can perform and on which aphasic errors appear. This method shortens testing procedures and at the same time gives the examiner a reasonable sample of behavior to observe in each language modality. It automatically selects the best tests for each patient.

2

Auditory Disturbances

An auditory factor did not emerge on factor analysis of the Minnesota Test [10]. All auditory tests loaded heavily on a general language factor that crossed all language modalities and rejected nonlanguage tests. There could be no stronger evidence for the importance of auditory processes in language than this finding, indicating as it does that the two processes are essentially inseparable.

If patients with mild aphasia show no impairment on any of the tests in Section A (Auditory Disturbances) of the Minnesota Test, it is necessary to go beyond the confines of the instrument and ascertain if they experience difficulty in any of their accustomed listening activities. Some patients report difficulty in following a conversation with several participants, or in following a newscast on the radio, a verbal report, a lecture, or a sermon. The examiner can usually demonstrate this impairment by reading additional factual paragraphs aloud, of gradually increasing length, and asking the patient to retell the content. Tests such as this have not been included in the Minnesota Test because overlap with normal performance is extensive unless subjects are carefully matched for age, intelligence, interests, and educational and cultural background. It would be significant if a lawyer could not follow testimony presented in court, or a doctor a case history reported in a staff conference, although neither might be intelligible to a layman.

Differential Diagnosis of Aphasia

Tests for auditory disturbances should be supplemented by pure tone audiometry to determine hearing acuity. There is ordinarily no correlation between hearing loss and aphasic impairment in understanding spoken language, but if hearing loss is present it must be taken into account in order to interpret test results accurately.

The Ammons *Full-Range Picture Vocabulary Test* is useful for indicating the extent of reduction of auditory vocabulary comprehension in aphasia, and is sensitive to increments that occur with recovery [9]. It gives the examiner a convenient method of estimating the discrepancy between the existing level of vocabulary comprehension and the level one would predict from the educational and vocational achievement of the patient.

(Sources for all supplementary tests cited in this volume are listed on page 108.)

TESTS INCLUDED IN SECTION A OF THE MINNESOTA TEST

Section A contains nine tests for auditory impairment. Table 5 lists these tests in order of difficulty as defined by the percentage of aphasic subjects making errors on each test, and presents additional data for aphasic and nonaphasic subjects. Standard deviations are large, for aphasic test distributions are characteristically J-shaped or U-shaped instead of normal curves. Nonaphasic subjects made occasional random errors compatible with transient inattention or distraction, or perhaps reflecting mild hearing or memory loss in some of the older subjects. No nonaphasic subject presented the consistent error pattern characteristic of aphasic patients.

The nine auditory tests were constructed to show not only how much the aphasic patient understands of what he hears, but why auditory comprehension breaks down when it does. On completion of auditory testing the examiner should be able to determine which of the following conditions the patient's behavior reflected:

1. Hearing loss (audiometric examination).
2. Impaired auditory discrimination (Tests 2, 3).
3. Reduction of vocabulary comprehension (Test 1, Ammons).
4. Reduction of auditory retention span (Tests 4, 6, 8, 9).

Table 5. Tests for Auditory Disturbances: Means, Standard Deviations, Median Scores, and Percentage of Subjects Making Errors [a]

Test	No.	Mean	SD	Median	Percentage of Subjects Making Errors
1. Recognizing common words					
Aphasics	157	1.48	2.73	0	33
Nonaphasics	50	0.00	0.00	0	0
2. Discriminating between paired words					
Aphasics	31	1.23	2.11	0	48
Nonaphasics	30	0.13	0.30	0	13
3. Recognizing letters					
Aphasics	75	5.88	7.43	3	61
Nonaphasics	50	0.00	0.00	0	0
4. Identifying items named serially					
Aphasics	157	2.68	2.42	2	66
Nonaphasics	50	0.02	0.14	0	2
5. Understanding sentences					
Aphasics	51	2.43	2.45	2	78
Nonaphasics	30	0.17	0.38	0	17
6. Following directions					
Aphasics	75	3.36	3.14	4	79
Nonaphasics	50	0.02	0.14	0	2
7. Understanding a paragraph					
Aphasics	75	2.48	2.14	2	80
Nonaphasics	50	0.42	0.92	0	42
8. Repeating digits (2–7)					
Aphasics	75	3.68	1.74	3	95
Nonaphasics	50	0.50	0.71	0	38
9. Repeating sentences					
Aphasics	75	3.89	1.98	4	96
Nonaphasics	50	0.10	0.36	0	8

[a] The data here, and in later tables reporting figures for aphasia patients as a group, do not include those for the 17 auditory and 7 dysfluent patients tested between 1965 and 1970 (see page 23). Data for them are given in italic type where diagnostic groups are compared.

The tests for sentence and paragraph comprehension are not diagnostic, but are included to give the examiner a general idea of how much the patient understands of what he hears. They do not test retention span, since subjects may respond by associations between the question and random words or phrases they manage to grasp. Although such patients make errors, the attempt to respond usually indicates that they are making maximal use of the information they receive, and are sometimes able to integrate it in a plausible manner. This usually indicates intact personality within the limitations of the aphasic deficit.

Test 1. Recognizing Common Words

This is the easiest of the auditory tests. It has high prognostic value, since it discriminates remarkably well between irreversible patients, who do not recover functional language, and subjects in the other diagnostic categories, who have a more favorable prognosis. The nonaphasic subjects tested made no errors on this test.

Irreversible subjects tended to make random responses or associative errors (boy for girl, dog for cat, etc.). Patients with impaired auditory perception also made errors on Test 1. These subjects usually either responded quickly and accurately or behaved as though they had not heard the word. They frequently looked bewildered, asked to have the word repeated, or indicated by words or gestures that they did not know what the examiner said.

On factor analysis Test 1 had the highest loading on stimulus equivalence (.61). The recognition that a perceived pattern represents a meaningful abstraction of experience is the essence of the symbolic process. Helen Keller described this moment of insight beautifully. She felt a stream of cold water on her hand, and her teacher traced the word *water* on her palm. She realized joyfully that everything had a name by which it could be remembered, so that she could think about it whenever she wished. Probably for most of us, a succession of simultaneous occurrences of words and events resulted in the gradual establishment of verbal equivalences we take for granted. This is too bad in a way, for it is a process that enriches experience but requires critical awareness as well, as many semanticists have pointed out.

The next highest loading was on the language factor (.49) and on spatial (.40) and visual factors (.38), since Test 1 used visual stimuli, which are spatially organized patterns. The extent to which visual or spatial impairment influenced the performance of a given subject can be inferred from his performance on matching tests.

28

Test 1 correlated most highly with matching pictures* (.92), identifying items named serially (.82), matching printed to spoken words (.82), reading comprehension, paragraph (.80), oral reading (.80), naming pictures (.79), following directions (.79), reading rate (.79), the Ammons Test (.78), matching words to pictures (.77), and writing words to visual* (.77) and to auditory stimulation* (.75). Thus it is clearly a language as well as an auditory test.

Test 2. Discriminating between Paired Words

Discriminating between pairs of words is essentially a test for phoneme discrimination. Tests that used phonemes in isolation or in nonsense syllables were discarded after unsatisfactory clinical trials, as were tests that required aphasic subjects to indicate if two stimuli were alike or different. Many patients responded adversely to tests that used meaningless materials. Some subjects refused the test or made minimal responses, saying apologetically, "I didn't have much schooling." It was frequently impossible to determine if patients failed because they could not discriminate between the given phonemes, because they did not understand the test instructions, because they could not retain sound patterns and instructions simultaneously, or because they found the task threatening for some other reason. Using common words facilitates perception and ensures maximal responses.

Items that tended to be failed by subjects with high-frequency hearing losses have been eliminated. Twenty-six out of 30 nonaphasic subjects made no errors on the test, while four subjects made one error each.

It is similarly probable that any aphasic subject might miss one or two of the 24 items without special significance. Four errors, however, represented one, and seven errors represented two standard deviations from the mean score obtained by aphasic subjects. Patients who made four or more errors had all been diagnosed as having partial auditory imperception. The test thus appears to be successful in identifying subjects with severe auditory involvement.

* Note that throughout this volume an asterisk denotes a test originally included in the series but not part of the published instrument.

Differential Diagnosis of Aphasia

Preliminary findings indicate that difficulty in discriminating between phonemes, as identified by this test, is an important aspect of auditory impairment for some patients. Aphasics with intermittent auditory imperception made more errors than any other group except irreversibles on this test.

This test was not included on factor analysis since it was in experimental form when the factor analysis was performed.

Test 3. Recognizing Letters

Sixty-one per cent of aphasic subjects and no nonaphasics made errors in pointing to letters of the alphabet named in random order. The kinds of errors subjects make have diagnostic significance.

The first common error is confusion between letters associated through serial order or between letters used relatively infrequently in English. Thus patients pointed to *g* for *f*, to *i* for *h*, or to *x* for *z*. These errors appear to be like the confusions between words with high-strength associational linkages such as *chair* and *table*, or *man* and *woman*. They tend to be made by patients with the fewest total errors.

A second common error is confusion between letters whose names sound alike, such as *b c d g p t v, a j k h, i y, f s x*, and *q u*. These are errors of auditory discrimination. Most aphasic patients make some errors of this kind initially. Consistent and persistent confusions of this kind indicate severe impairment of auditory perception.

The test groups letters in such a manner as to maximize the demands upon auditory discrimination, except on Card 1-1 (see *Card Materials* [6]) which uses dissimilar items. Card 1-1 is therefore the easiest and Card 1-4 the most difficult for patients with severe impairment of auditory discrimination.

Test 3 had its highest factor loading on the general language factor (.67), with a significant loading also on the visual factor (.58), since visual stimuli were used. It correlated most highly with writing letters to dictation (.91), written spelling (.90), and producing written sentences (.90). Correlation coefficients above .85 were obtained between Test 3 and matching printed to spoken words (.89), writing sentences to dictation (.88), identifying items named seri-

PERFORMANCE ON RECOGNIZING LETTERS

Diagnostic Group	Number	Mean	Percentage of Subjects Making Errors
Simple	12	0.33	25
Visual	8	2.00	63
Persisting Dysfluency [a]	*7*	*0.29*	*14*
Scattered findings	26	4.00	50
Sensorimotor	11	4.00	73
Auditory (1)	6	12.00	100
Auditory (2) [a]	*17*	*12.65*	*94*
Irreversible	12	16.75	100
Total aphasic subjects	75	5.88 (SD = 7.43)	61
Total nonaphasic subjects..	50	0.00	0

[a] Not included in the totals.

ally (.87), following directions (.87), naming pictures (.87), simple numerical combinations (.87), writing words to auditory* (.87) and to visual stimulation* (.86), and defining words (.86).

The means obtained for subjects in the various diagnostic groups are of some interest. They are shown in the tabulation. The use of visual materials clearly made pointing to letters a harder task for visual than for simple aphasia patients. The severe language reduction in the sensorimotor group is offset by the visual involvement in the scattered-findings group, so that the average performances of these groups approximate one another. Irreversible subjects performed minimally, while subjects classified as having intermittent auditory imperception performed more like subjects in the irreversible group than the remainder of the aphasic population.

Test 4. Identifying Items Named Serially

Identifying items named serially tests auditory retention span for subjects who cannot repeat. Sixty-six per cent of aphasic subjects made errors on the test, while the sum of errors for the 50 nonaphasic subjects was one.

The test had its highest loading on the general language factor (.67), with the second highest loading on the visual factor (.56). It correlated most highly with following directions (.93). Correlations above .85 were obtained with recognizing letters (.87), matching

31

Differential Diagnosis of Aphasia

printed to spoken words (.87), reading comprehension, paragraph (.86), naming pictures (.86), oral reading (.85), giving biographical information (.85), and writing sentences to dictation (.85). The correlation with repeating digits was .81.

In general the scores of persisting dysfluency, simple aphasia, and visual patients were slightly above the mean for all aphasic subjects, while the scores of subjects in the sensorimotor and scattered-findings groups were slightly below. Most irreversible subjects missed all items, while subjects with intermittent auditory imperception only slightly exceeded the performance of irreversible patients, with a mean of 4.33 out of six possible errors.

Test 5. Understanding Sentences

Seventy-eight per cent of aphasic subjects made errors on understanding sentences read by the examiner. The range of errors was 0–8, and the mean error was 2.43 (SD = 2.45). Twenty-five out of 30 nonaphasics made no errors, while five subjects made one error each.

Most aphasic errors result from reduction of verbal retention span. For example, with a sentence like "Does everyone put money in the bank?" the patient who cannot retain the entire sequence of words in his mind tends to respond to *money* and *bank*. This is a meaningful association, so the patient responds affirmatively, although further questioning may reveal that he knows everyone does not have a bank account. This is not necessarily the case with a sentence such as "Should children disobey their parents?" where an erroneous response usually results from a failure to distinguish between *obey* and *disobey*. There is evidence for an acquiescent response bias even stronger in aphasic than in normal subjects, so the most productive items are those requiring negative responses.

This test was not included in the factor analysis, since it was in experimental form when the factor analysis was performed.

Test-retest results were available for 17 aphasic subjects, who made a total of 63 errors on admission to the Aphasia Section of the Minneapolis Veterans Administration Hospital, and 30 errors at time of discharge, with respective means of 3.70 and 1.76, indicating that improvement occurred on this as on other auditory tests.

Test 6. Following Directions

Seventy-nine per cent of aphasic subjects made errors in following directions, while the sum of errors for 50 nonaphasic subjects was one. The mean numbers of errors in the diagnostic categories, shown in the tabulation, are again revealing.

Test 6 contributes little to understanding patients with minimal or mild aphasia, and can be omitted for these subjects. It has been retained because it permits the examiner to make meaningful observations of the behavior of patients with severe aphasia. The use of common objects helps to orient the patient to the task. There are few subjects who do not respond to the shortest and simplest directions in some manner. The patient may touch the bell instead of ringing it, but this shows that partial comprehension has occurred. On the other hand, the patient who cannot respond to such a simple direction as "Put the penny in the cup" demonstrates a degree of auditory impairment that may give insight into much of his habitual behavior.

Following directions had its highest factor loading on language (.71), and the second highest on the visual factor (.59). It cor-

PERFORMANCE ON FOLLOWING DIRECTIONS

Diagnostic Group	Number	Mean	Percentage of Subjects Making Errors
Simple	12	0.75	42
Visual	8	1.25	63
Persisting Dysfluency [a]	*7*	*0.43*	*29*
Scattered findings	26	2.15	77
Sensorimotor	11	4.27	100
Auditory (1)	6	6.50	100
Auditory (2) [a]	*17*	*6.24*	*100*
Irreversible	12	7.58	100
Total aphasic subjects.....	75	3.36 (SD = 3.14)	79
Total nonaphasic subjects..	50	0.02 (SD = 0.14)	2

[a] Not included in the totals.

33

Differential Diagnosis of Aphasia

related most highly with identifying items named serially (.93). Correlations above .85 were obtained with oral reading (.91), matching printed to spoken words (.89), giving biographical information (.88), writing words to visual stimulation* (.88), naming pictures (.87), recognizing letters named in random order (.87), written spelling (.87), producing written sentences (.86), and understanding a paragraph read by the examiner (.85).

Test 7. Understanding a Paragraph

Eighty per cent of aphasic subjects made errors on paragraph comprehension, with a mean error of 2.48. Forty-two per cent of nonaphasic subjects made errors with a mean of 0.42.

Performance by diagnostic categories is summarized in the tabulation. As on most of the higher level tests, there is overlap in the performance of aphasic and nonaphasic subjects, particularly nonaphasic subjects in the older age groups. The examiner noted that many of the older subjects commented that they could not remember as well as they used to. She also observed a tendency for older subjects to confabulate rather than answer a question directly.

The median error was 2 for aphasic and 0 for nonaphasic subjects. Only one nonaphasic subject, who made three errors, exceeded the mean error of the aphasic subjects.

PERFORMANCE ON UNDERSTANDING A PARAGRAPH

Diagnostic Group	Number	Mean	Percentage of Subjects Making Errors
Simple	12	1.92	67
Visual	8	1.13	50
Persisting Dysfluency [a]	7	0.57	29
Scattered findings	26	2.81	73
Sensorimotor	11	2.55	100
Auditory (1)	6	5.50	100
Auditory (2) [a]	17	3.24	82
Irreversible	12	5.00	100
Total aphasic subjects	75	2.48 (SD = 2.14)	80
Total nonaphasic subjects..	50	0.42 (SD = 0.92)	42

[a] Not included in the totals.

Auditory patients made fewer errors than one would expect from the performance on tests with shorter auditory stimuli because they are able to get more clues from longer material.

The test had its highest factor loading on language (.61). The second highest loading was on the visual factor (.36). This loading was lower than the visual loading on tests that used visual materials, but it may indicate that visualization of narrated events played some role in responses.

Paragraph comprehension correlated most highly with repeating sentences (.76). Correlation coefficients above .70 were obtained with repeating digits (.74), completing sentences (.74), matching printed to spoken words (.72), naming the days of the week (.72), defining words (.71), giving biographical information (.71), describing a picture (.70), and writing sentences to dictation (.70).

Test 8. Repeating Digits

Test 8 requires straightforward repetition of digits in series ranging from two to seven. Only four of 75 aphasic subjects succeeded in repeating seven digits, and none succeeded in repeating eight, so seven was used as the cut-off point. This slightly reduced the mean for nonaphasic subjects, a few of whom succeeded in repeating eight digits. The mean number of digits repeated correctly was 3.06 for the aphasic subjects, and 6.50 for 50 nonaphasic subjects.

Sixty-two per cent of nonaphasic subjects compared with 5 per cent of aphasic subjects succeeded in repeating seven digits. Subjects under 50 years of age exceeded the performance of subjects over 50 in the nonaphasic series, with 74 per cent of the younger subjects, compared with 55 per cent of the older group, repeating seven digits. All nonaphasic subjects repeated a series of five digits correctly, while only 29 per cent of aphasic subjects were able to do this well.

The mean number of digits repeated by aphasic subjects in each of the diagnostic categories is shown above. It should be noted that these means represent the average number of digits subjects repeated correctly. The means given in Table 5 represent the mean number

Differential Diagnosis of Aphasia

NUMBER AND MEAN NUMBER OF DIGITS
REPEATED CORRECTLY

Diagnostic Group	Number	Mean Number of Digits
Simple	12	4.75
Visual	8	4.63
Persisting Dysfluency[a] ...	7	5.00
Scattered findings	26	3.88
Sensorimotor	11	2.27
Auditory (1)	6	0.00
Auditory (2)[a]	17	1.06
Irreversible	12	0.83
Total aphasic subjects ...	75	3.06 (SD = 2.12)
Total nonaphasic subjects	50	6.50 (SD = 0.62)

[a] Not included in the totals.

of errors (0–6) made by aphasic and nonaphasic subjects on the test.

For subjects who can repeat, repetition of digits forward is a precise test of auditory retention span, and a test that is sensitive enough to reflect increments that occur with recovery.

Repeating digits in reverse order has been deleted in the published test since performance of normal subjects is extremely variable, and it is not clear what this test measures.

Repeating digits had its highest loading on the general language factor (.89). The second highest loading was on the visual factor (.31), indicating, perhaps, that some subjects visualized numbers as they were read. The test correlated most highly with repeating sentences (.98). Correlation coefficients above .90 were obtained with most language tests, and above .80 with writing a paragraph (.88), producing written sentences (.88), writing sentences to dictation (.87), following directions (.82), and identifying items named serially (.81).

Test 9. Repeating Sentences

Like repeating digits, repeating sentences of progressive length is a test of auditory retention span. Both tests have been retained because repetition of sentences does a little better in discriminating

36

between nonaphasic subjects and subjects with mild aphasia, as evidenced by the fact that only 8 per cent of nonaphasic subjects made any errors on repeating sentences, whereas 38 per cent could not repeat seven digits. Repeating sentences also helps to give the examiner an idea of the length of functional language units the patient can retain.

Like repeating digits, repeating sentences had its highest loading on the general language factor (.94), and the second highest loading on the visual factor (.30). It correlated most highly with repeating digits (.98). Correlation coefficients above .90 were obtained with most of the verbal tests and oral spelling, and above .80 with oral reading (.86), following directions (.82), and writing a paragraph (.82).

3

Visual and Reading Disturbances

Before testing reading it is necessary to ascertain that the patient can see the materials. Patients who use glasses for reading should not be tested without them. Reliable information about visual problems can frequently be obtained by questioning the patient. Sometimes, however, a patient who has difficulty discriminating between learned visual patterns believes he cannot see them. Reduction of acuity is usually related to pre-traumatic visual defects in aphasic patients, rather than to cerebral involvement of visual processes. Often, however, the patient's vision changes during the course of an illness, and he will benefit from having his eyes refracted by a competent ophthalmologist. Occasionally, also, in cases of head injury or tumor, there may be reduction of acuity, secondary to involvement of the optic nerve.

Many patients compensate unconsciously for visual field limitations by turning the head, but some do not and tend to ignore words or objects to one side or the other. Patients with right or left homonymous hemianopia have limited vision in corresponding halves of each eye. Sometimes, however, they report that they cannot see well with one eye or the other, which is an understandable misconception. Occasionally an aphasic patient complains of diplopia, or double vision. In such cases an ophthalmologist should be consulted about the advisability of covering one eye.

38

Visual and Reading Disturbances

Some aphasic patients complain of blurring or of intermittent clouding of vision. These patients frequently omit words randomly in reading, because they do not see them as they scan the line. Some aphasic patients have impaired perception of directionality and of spatial relationships. Subjects with visual field defects, intermittent clouding, or impaired spatial discrimination may all have difficulty following a line of print and keeping their place while reading.

An ophthalmologist is often unable to obtain reliable refraction or visual fields with an aphasic patient because the patient cannot cooperate adequately in testing. It is usually helpful for the examiner to make as many observations as possible about the conditions under which the patient sees. A patient considered cortically blind once pointed out and named a minuscule object in the background of a picture, which the examiner had never observed. Another referred for inability to recognize objects had no difficulty when the examiner held objects on the palm of one hand and allowed the patient to manipulate the position of the arm until the entire object became visible.

In summary, the aphasic patient may have difficulty in performing reading tests because of reduced visual acuity, blurring, intermittent clouding of vision, diplopia, a visual field defect, or spatial disorientation. None of these are aphasic disabilities, since any of them can and do exist without aphasia, as well as when aphasia is present. They are conditions, however, that sometimes make it difficult or impossible to get a reliable estimate of reading ability.

SUPPLEMENTARY TESTS

The Gates *Primary* and *Advanced Primary Tests for Word Recognition* require subjects to match words to pictures. Severely aphasic patients frequently perform better than one might expect on these tests, showing ability to make visual discriminations and retention of limited reading vocabulary. Errors tend to increase as word frequency decreases and as word length increases. These are useful tests for securing maximal performance and indicating discrepancy between obtained performance and previous achievement inferred from educational and vocational history. The Atwell and Wells

Differential Diagnosis of Aphasia

Wide-Range Vocabulary Test serves a similar purpose for highly literate patients with mild aphasia.

The *Iowa Silent Reading Tests for Vocabulary, Sentence Comprehension, and Paragraph Comprehension* are also useful for showing reading impairment in subjects with mild aphasia. A characteristic aphasic pattern is a comparatively low score on paragraph comprehension, somewhat better performance on sentence comprehension, with the highest score obtained on vocabulary. In other words, errors increase as stimuli increase in length. This pattern is useful for discriminating aphasic impairment from impairment reflecting other conditions such as depression, mental deficiency, or low educational level.

The *Gray Oral Reading Tests* are sensitive to improvement of dysarthric conditions.

TESTS INCLUDED IN SECTION B OF THE MINNESOTA TEST

There are nine tests for visual and reading impairment in Section B (Visual and Reading Disturbances) of the Minnesota Test. Means, standard deviations, median scores, and percentage of subjects making errors are shown for aphasic and nonaphasic subjects in Table 6.

There are two matching tests, matching forms and matching letters. These tests are useful for screening out gross impairment of visual and spatial discrimination. Tests for matching words to pictures and matching printed to spoken words enable the examiner to observe whether the visual cue (picture) or the auditory cue (the spoken word) is more effective in stimulating word recognition. Both tests are constructed to permit the examiner to determine if errors result chiefly from impaired auditory, visual, or semantic discrimination. In other words, the tests ask if the patient shows a particular tendency to confuse words that sound alike, words that look alike, or words associated in meaning.

Sentence and paragraph comprehension tests show the level at which reading comprehension breaks down. The patient who recognizes most common words but does poorly on sentence comprehension is usually showing inability to recognize and integrate the struc-

40

Visual and Reading Disturbances

Table 6. Tests for Visual and Reading Disturbances: Means, Standard
Deviations, Median Scores, and Percentage of Subjects Making Errors

Test	No.	Mean	SD	Median	Percentage of Subjects Making Errors
1. Matching forms					
Aphasics	157	0.25	0.17	0	14
Nonaphasics	100	0.00	0.00	0	0
2. Matching letters					
Aphasics	75	0.84	2.81	0	23
Nonaphasics	50	0.00	0.00	0	0
3. Matching words to pictures					
Aphasics	75	3.40	6.99	1	57
Nonaphasics	50	0.00	0.00	0	0
4. Matching printed to spoken words					
Aphasics	75	4.69	7.10	2	68
Nonaphasics	50	0.00	0.00	0	0
5. Reading comprehension, sentences					
Aphasics	54	1.85	1.88	1	70
Nonaphasics	30	0.10	0.30	0	10
6. Reading rate, sentences					
Aphasics	75	3.93	2.24	5	91
Nonaphasics	50	0.38	0.70	0	28
7. Reading comprehension, paragraph					
Aphasics	75	4.44	2.78	4	93
Nonaphasics	50	1.86	1.55	1.5	74
8. Oral reading, words					
Aphasics	75	6.69	5.73	6	81
Nonaphasics	50	0.08	0.44	0	2
9. Oral reading, sentences					
Aphasics	75	27.99	25.41	18	87
Nonaphasics	50	0.10	0.44	0	20

tural units of a sentence, and usually inability to retain a sufficiently
long string of words to do so. He tends to respond to random words
that convey meaning to him and to guess at the answer. A patient
who performs reasonably well on sentences but breaks down on paragraph comprehension is also showing reduction of verbal retention
span, but on a higher level. He loses much of the content because
by the time he has finished reading one sentence he has forgotten
what he read in the sentence before.

Oral reading tests are included chiefly to enable the examiner to

41

observe the kind of reading errors the subject makes, in order to diagnose reading disability with more confidence.

At the end of this test section, the examiner should be able to determine not only how much the patient can read, but why reading breaks down when it does. He should know which of the following conditions are present, and how much they contribute to the observed reading disability:

1. Visual involvement
   a. reduction of acuity (observations of test behavior, verified by ophthalmological examination)
   b. visual field defect (observations of test behavior, verified by neurological examination)
   c. spatial disorientation (Tests 1, 2)
   d. impaired pattern discrimination (Tests 1, 2)
2. Language impairment
   a. reduction of reading vocabulary (Tests 3, 4)
   b. reduction of verbal retention span (Tests 5, 7)

The examiner should remember that reading can be virtually nonfunctional when no involvement of visual processes is present. The sensorimotor subjects, for example, usually perform much like simple aphasic subjects on matching tests, although reading is extremely limited because of severe reduction of language.

Test 1. Matching Forms

Fourteen per cent of aphasic and no nonaphasic subjects made errors in matching forms. On factor analysis this test had its highest loading on visuospatial perception (.84), and the second highest loading on recognition of stimulus equivalence (.43). It correlated most highly with matching letters (.97).

Correlations of .70 or above were obtained with long division (.78), copying Greek letters (.77), reproducing letters (.75), copying forms* (.72), recognizing common words spoken by the examiner (.72), and assembling the Wechsler manikin (.72). Two matching tests were eliminated, matching colors and matching pictures, because few subjects made errors on them. It is not necessary to use

42

matching forms with all subjects. This test was retained in the Minnesota instrument in order to have an easy test on which severely impaired patients could perform. All subjects in the test series passed some items. Experiencing initial success makes it easier for the patient to attempt harder tasks, and this helps secure maximal performance. It is important, also, that the examiner observe what the severely impaired patient is able to do. If he performs well enough to indicate that he understands the task and is cooperating to the best of his ability, the examiner is able to determine the nature of observed disruptions of performance with more confidence.

Test 2. Matching Letters

Twenty-three per cent of aphasic and no nonaphasic subjects made errors in matching letters. The test had its highest factor loading (.61) on the visuospatial factor, and next highest (.54) on recognition of stimulus equivalence.

Matching letters correlated most highly with matching forms (.97). The next highest correlations were with recognizing common words spoken by the examiner (.65), matching words to pictures (.63), assembling the Wechsler manikin (.60), copying Greek letters (.59), and making change (.59).

Letters were selected and grouped to maximize confusions resulting from impaired visuospatial discrimination. The most common errors made in both reading and writing by patients with impaired pattern perception are confusions between $W M$, $H N Z V$, $F E$, $L J$, $t f$, $p d b q$, and $u n h r$. However, because of the size of the letters, the fact that only one discrimination is demanded at a time, and the continuous availability of stimuli, this is a comparatively easy test and tends to reflect only relatively gross impairment. Scattered-findings and irreversible patients made the highest percentages of errors in matching letters.

Test 3. Matching Words to Pictures

Fifty-seven per cent of aphasic and no nonaphasic subjects made errors in matching words to pictures. This test also had its highest factor loading on visuospatial discrimination (.54), but the next

Differential Diagnosis of Aphasia

highest loading was on the general language factor (.45), which was slightly higher than the loading on stimulus equivalence (.43).

Matching words to pictures correlated most highly (.89) with matching printed to spoken words. Correlations above .75 were secured with long division (.87), reading rate (.80), writing words to visual stimulation* (.78), recognizing common words spoken by the examiner (.77), making change (.77), recognizing letters named in random order (.75), and reading comprehension, paragraph (.75).

Since patients select one of two words to match the picture, it is possible to choose the correct word by chance, and this undoubtedly happens. However, mean errors for diagnostic groups indicate clearly that more than chance factors influence performance, as may be seen in the tabulation.

Words are paired so that choices occur between words associated in meaning, words with similar visual patterns, words with similar auditory patterns, and random pairs. Previous studies [8] have shown that confusions between words associated in meaning are the "best" errors, in that they tend to be made by subjects who make the fewest total errors on vocabulary tests. Conversely, confusions between random pairs are the "worst" errors, in that they are made by subjects who make the most total errors. Visual and auditory confusions, on the other hand, did not correlate with total errors, but

PERFORMANCE ON MATCHING WORDS TO PICTURES

Diagnostic Group	Number	Mean	Percentage of Subjects Making Errors
Simple	12	0.25	25
Visual	8	0.89	50
Persisting Dysfluency[a]	7	*0.14*	*14*
Scattered findings	26	2.38	85
Sensorimotor	11	1.45	73
Auditory (1)	6	6.83	83
Auditory (2)[a]	17	*3.82*	*76*
Irreversible	12	10.50	100
Total aphasic subjects	75	3.40 (SD = 6.99)	57
Total nonaphasic subjects	50	0.00	0

[a] Not included in the totals.

tended to be made most frequently by subjects who showed other evidence of specific visual or auditory impairment.

Most subjects, of course, make more than one kind of error, and any patient may make errors of any kind. It is only when a preponderance of one kind of error is present that error type has diagnostic significance. In the present series the highest percentages of semantic errors occurred in simple aphasia and visual; the highest percentages of auditory errors in sensorimotor and in aphasia with intermittent auditory imperception; the highest percentage of visual errors in visual and scattered-findings patients; and the highest percentage of random errors in scattered-findings and irreversible patients. No random errors occurred in simple aphasia, visual, dysfluent, or sensorimotor patients. These results were all as predicted on the basis of previous studies.

Test 4. Matching Printed to Spoken Words

Sixty-eight per cent of aphasic and no nonaphasic patients made errors in matching printed to spoken words. Highest factor loadings were on language (.63) and visual (.52) factors, while loadings on visuospatial (.33) and stimulus equivalence factors (.31) were relatively low. Factor 2, the visual factor, included both recognition and recall of learned visual patterns.

Matching printed to spoken words correlated most highly with recognizing letters named in random order (.89), matching words to pictures (.89), following directions (.89), oral reading (.88), writing words to visual stimulation* (.86), writing letters to dictation (.86), identifying items named serially (.86), and writing sentences to dictation (.85).

In general aphasic subjects averaged more errors in matching printed to spoken words than in matching the same words to pictures. Differences between means were greatest, however, for sensorimotor and irreversible patients, indicating that the picture helped these groups more than hearing the word. Individual visual subjects reversed the over-all trend, and were sometimes markedly more successful when an auditory stimulus was presented and they did not have to depend on visual stimuli alone. In addition scattered-findings

45

patients reversed the general trend, in that 85 per cent made errors in matching words to pictures, while only 58 per cent made errors in matching printed to spoken words.

Distribution of error types by diagnostic groups was almost erratic on this test. Simple aphasia, visual, sensorimotor, and auditory patients all averaged more auditory errors than any other kind, while scattered-findings and irreversible patients averaged slightly more visual errors. These results probably reflect the double hazard presented aphasic subjects by a task that requires the patient to perceive an auditory pattern and retain it long enough to make a choice that requires further fine discriminations.

Test 5. Reading Comprehension, Sentences

Seventy per cent of aphasic and 10 per cent of nonaphasic subjects made errors in reading simple sentences for comprehension. Three of the 30 nonaphasic subjects missed one sentence each; the sentence missed was different in each case. On factor analysis, sentence comprehension had a loading of .52 on the language and .48 on the visual factor.

Sentence comprehension correlated most highly with oral reading (.86), reading comprehension, paragraph (.85), writing sentences to dictation (.83), writing words to visual* (.81) and to auditory stimulation (.80), and following directions (.80).

Sentences most frequently missed by aphasic subjects were these: (1) Can anyone get a license to drive a car? (2) Is summer colder than winter? (3) Are there many railroads in the United States?

No nonaphasic subjects missed these sentences. The first two illustrate the aphasic tendency to respond to meaningful associations, such as *license-car*, and *colder-winter*, when the patient is unable to read or retain the entire sentence. Why almost a quarter of the aphasic subjects should have missed the third sentence is less clear. If nonaphasics had missed it, one should have suspected a judgment factor related to publicized reductions of passenger services. Although *railroads* can scarcely be considered an archaic term, it has been changed to *highways* in the present edition.

46

Visual and Reading Disturbances

Test 6. Reading Rate, Sentences

Reading rate is operationally defined as the time in seconds required to complete Test 5. Reading rate had the highest factor loadings on visual (.59) and language factors (.49). Reading rate thus seems to be a function of visual perception and meaningfulness of language.

The highest obtained correlations were with oral reading (.85) and reading comprehension, paragraph (.84). Other significant correlations were with identifying items named serially (.82), matching words to pictures (.80), writing words to visual* (.80) and to auditory stimulation* (.79), matching printed to spoken words (.78), written spelling (.78), following directions (.77), naming pictures (.75), and reading comprehension, sentences (.73). The correlation with sentence comprehension indicates some relationship between speed and accuracy, although not complete overlap of the two reading skills on this task.

Nonaphasic subjects under 50 years of age averaged 60 seconds to complete the task, while those over 50 required 92 seconds. The mean for all nonaphasic subjects was 77 seconds, compared with 202 seconds for aphasic subjects. The time range for nonaphasic subjects was from 20 to 180 seconds with the median at 60, compared with 46 to 660 seconds for aphasic subjects with the median falling between 175 and 182 seconds. Only two aphasic subjects completed the task in less than 60 seconds. No nonaphasic subject required as long as the average aphasic.

Test 7. Reading Comprehension, Paragraph

Paragraph comprehension is the most difficult of the reading tests, with 93 per cent of aphasic and 74 per cent of nonaphasic subjects making errors. The mean error for aphasic subjects was 4.44, compared with 1.86 for nonaphasic subjects.

The paragraph is based on a newspaper item, which was rewritten to reduce sentence length and simplify paragraph structure. The paragraph does not go beyond easy adult reading level. The questions are straightforward and factual, and subjects are told to read the paragraph as many times as they wish, and to go back to look for the

47

Differential Diagnosis of Aphasia

right answer if they are not sure. The test is untimed. The score does not depend on memory or on reading rate per se. What is tested is the patient's ability to get meaning from the printed page. In spite of the fact that the test is not difficult enough to reveal reading impairment in highly literate subjects with mild aphasia, there is considerable overlap between the performance of subjects with mild aphasia and nonaphasic subjects with limited education. This emphasizes the necessity for using supplementary tests to obtain a test ceiling when necessary, and of comparing the performance of each aphasic subject with the reading level one would expect from his educational and vocational history. Thus one subject might make several errors on this test, and the examiner be willing to infer nothing more than that reading ability is probably compatible with educational level. Another subject might make no errors, but more extensive testing reveal that aphasic impairment exists, and the patient himself be very much aware of a reading handicap. He may report, for example, that he no longer enjoys reading because he has to go back to reread constantly in order to get the meaning, or that he cannot remember what he reads. Standardized timed tests usually support these statements.

Paragraph comprehension, like sentence comprehension, had its highest factor loadings on visual (.71) and language (.48) factors. The highest correlations were with following directions (.90), producing written sentences (.88), oral reading (.87), matching pictures* (.86), writing sentences to dictation (.86), identifying items named serially (.86), writing words to visual* (.86) and to auditory stimulation* (.85), and reading comprehension, sentences (.85). The highest correlation supports the hypothesis that verbal retention span is an important dimension of reading comprehension in aphasia, since this test consists of items of gradually increasing length. This is also true of writing sentences to dictation and pointing to items named serially.

Test 8. Oral Reading, Words

Eighty-one per cent of aphasic compared with 2 per cent of nonaphasic subjects made errors reading words aloud. Nonaphasic ar-

48

PERFORMANCE ON ORAL READING, WORDS

Diagnostic Group	Number	Mean	Percentage of Subjects Making Errors
Simple	12	0.25	25
Visual	8	3.75	88
Persisting Dysfluency[a]	7	3.14	57
Scattered findings	26	4.88	85
Sensorimotor	11	10.18	100
Auditory (1)	6	9.33	100
Auditory (2)[a]	17	11.18	100
Irreversible	12	14.50	100
Total aphasic subjects	75	6.69 (SD = 5.73)	81
Total nonaphasic subjects	50	0.08 (SD = 0.44)	2

[a] Not included in the totals.

ticulation or pronunciation errors may occur as a result of absence of teeth, foreign accent, educational deficit, or, more rarely, a lifelong articulation impairment, such as a lisp. Aphasic errors tend to increase as a function of word frequency and word length determined by number of syllables.

Performance by diagnostic groups is summarized in the tabulation.

Test 9. Oral Reading, Sentences

Eighty-seven per cent of aphasic and 20 per cent of nonaphasic subjects made errors in reading sentences aloud. The mean error was 27.99 for aphasic and 0.10 for nonaphasic subjects.

Reading sentences orally had the highest factor loadings on language (.74) and visual (.50) factors. In marked comparison the loading on Factor 4, the only factor related to speech movements, was .01.

Test 9 correlated most highly with following directions (.91), naming pictures (.90), repeating digits (.88), matching printed to spoken words (.88), reading comprehension, paragraph (.87), defining words (.87), describing a picture (.87), oral spelling (.87), producing written sentences (.87), repeating sentences (.86), completing sentences (.86), naming days of the week (.86), giving biographical information (.86), writing words to auditory stimulation*

49

Differential Diagnosis of Aphasia

PERFORMANCE ON ORAL READING, SENTENCES

Diagnostic Group	Number	Mean	Percentage of Subjects Making Errors
Simple	12	1.67	25
Visual	11	17.50	85
Persisting Dysfluency[a]	7	9.29	43
Scattered findings	26	22.23	96
Sensorimotor	8	40.27	100
Auditory (1)	6	35.33	100
Auditory (2)[a]	17	25.65	100
Irreversible	12	58.83	100
Total aphasic subjects	75	27.99 (SD = 25.41)	87
Total nonaphasic subjects ..	50	0.10 (SD = 0.44)	20

[a] Not included in the totals.

(.86), identifying items named serially (.85), and reading rate (.85).

The tabulation summarizes performance by diagnostic groups.

Oral reading tests were included primarily to enable the examiner to observe the kind of reading difficulties a given patient encountered, as an aid to differential diagnosis of reading disabilities.

Mean errors were based on scores obtained by counting each word mispronounced, misread, or omitted as one error. On the present form each word not read correctly is counted as ½ error, to make the number of possible errors more consistent with other tests in this section.

4

Speech and Language Disturbances

SUPPLEMENTARY TESTS

It is sometimes desirable to use supplementary tests to explore disruptions of language in highly intelligent and literate patients with mild aphasia. This is particularly true when patients are followed for a period of years and re-examined at intervals. The pertinent question becomes whether the patient can return to an occupation that requires a high level of language competence or whether enough residual aphasia remains to contraindicate the attempt. It should be emphasized that depressed scores on intelligence tests usually reflect severity of aphasia, and marked changes in performance level occur during the course of recovery. Intelligence tests such as the *Wechsler Adult Intelligence Scale* and the *Revised Stanford-Binet Scales* are useful, however, for comparing the performance of aphasic subjects with that of a non-brain-injured population, in order to assess limitations and functional competence at a given time. Such tests should be administered by qualified examiners, the results cautiously interpreted, and conclusions guarded.

TESTS INCLUDED IN SECTION C OF THE MINNESOTA TEST

Table 7 lists the 15 tests contained in Section C (Speech and Language Disturbances) of the Minnesota instrument, with means,

Table 7. Tests for Speech and Language Disturbances: Means, Standard
Deviations, Median Scores, and Percentage of Subjects Making Errors

Test	No.	Mean	SD	Median	Percentage of Subjects Making Errors
Tests for Speech Movements					
1. Imitating gross movements					
Aphasics	75	0.72	1.86	0	36
Nonaphasics	50	0.00	0.00	0	0
2. Rapid alternating movements					
Aphasics	75	1.65	2.26	1	56
Nonaphasics	50	0.00	0.00	0	0
3. Repeating monosyllables					
Aphasics	75	8.00	3.27	3	61
Nonaphasics	50	0.08	0.31	0	4
4. Repeating phrases					
Aphasics	75	6.57	7.61	3	67
Nonaphasics	50	0.04	0.20	0	4
Tests for Language Disturbances					
5. Counting to 20					
Aphasics	157	2.84	3.87	0	40
Nonaphasics	100	0.00	0.00	0	0
6. Naming days of week					
Aphasics	157	2.35	3.14	0	43
Nonaphasics	100	0.00	0.00	0	0
7. Completing sentences					
Aphasics	75	1.81	2.83	0	43
Nonaphasics	50	0.00	0.00	0	0
8. Answering simple questions					
Aphasics	75	2.57	3.31	0	49
Nonaphasics	50	0.00	0.00	0	0
9. Giving biographical information					
Aphasics	75	5.63	6.10	3	64
Nonaphasics	50	0.00	0.00	0	0
10. Expressing ideas					
Aphasics	75	2.37	2.39	2	65
Nonaphasics	50	0.02	0.14	0	2
11. Producing sentences					
Aphasics	75	3.04	2.68	3	68
Nonaphasics	50	0.00	0.00	0	0
12. Describing picture					
Aphasics	75	3.16	2.13	3	84
Nonaphasics	50	0.00	0.00	0	0
13. Naming pictures					
Aphasics	75	8.45	7.62	6	85
Nonaphasics	50	0.00	0.00	0	0

Table 7. Continued

Test	No.	Mean	SD	Median	Percentage of Subjects Making Errors
14. Defining words					
Aphasics	75	6.08	3.66	7	89
Nonaphasics	50	0.60	1.07	0	32
15. Retelling paragraph					
Aphasics	75	4.59	1.63	5	99
Nonaphasics	50	0.74	1.31	0	28

standard deviations, median scores, and percentage of subjects making errors on each test, for aphasics and nonaphasics.

The first four tests involve speech movements and articulation patterns. A movement factor was clearly identified on factor analysis [10]. However, the factor loading on language approaches the loading on movements on the test for rapid alternating movements, and exceeds it on repetition of monosyllables (repetition of phrases was not included on factor analysis). The language loadings emphasize the learned character of movement patterns used in speech, and strongly suggest that articulation must be viewed in relation to integrity of language patterns as well as integrity of motor processes.

The easiest language tests are counting to 20 and naming the days of the week, which utilize highly overlearned language sequences. Although these tests are highly correlated (.94), both are included for their effectiveness in obtaining language responses in severe aphasia.

Sentence completion and response to questions are comparatively easy tests because strong associational linkages provided by given stimuli tend to evoke the correct response. Once the musculature is working, even irreversible subjects make some correct responses on these tests.

The remainder of the language tests increase in difficulty gradually, as more voluntary or more precise or longer responses are required. Naming pictures has been made a little more difficult on this than on earlier test forms by including less commonly used words, although none of the words used were missed by nonaphasic sub-

53

jects. Defining words is a difficult task for aphasic subjects because it requires that the patient have enough language to say the same thing another way. Retelling a paragraph is the most difficult test, since it is highly dependent upon verbal retention span. It unexpectedly proved to be a more difficult task for aphasic subjects than explaining proverbs, the test in earlier forms which it replaces.

Upon completion of Section C the examiner should be able to determine which of the following disabilities are present:

1. Dysarthria, defined as consistent impairment of articulation or fluency, not necessarily correlated with reduction of language. Dysarthria may reflect paralysis or paresis of the musculature, such as is found in bulbar poliomyelitis, in cerebral palsy, or in pseudobulbar disorders; or impaired coordination and control of motor processes, as in some cerebellar diseases. When dysarthria alone is present, reading, writing, and auditory comprehension are normal. (Tests 1, 4.)

2. Dysfluency, defined as impairment of articulation not correlated with reduction of language. This impairment is characterized by phonemic disintegration due to reduced proprioceptive information, but with auditory discrimination intact. The patient continually corrects, by ear, errors of placement. The aphasia is usually very mild or transient, while the dysfluency is persistent, and the patient must continually exert control over the speech musculature. (Tests 2, 3, 4.)

3. Sensorimotor impairment, without paralysis or paresis of the musculature. Sensorimotor impairment is characterized by phonemic disintegration in conjunction with reduced auditory and proprioceptive discrimination, and is correlated with over-all reduction of language. Frequently used words and phrases are usually produced normally as language is recovered. (Tests 2, 3, 4.)

4. Inconsistent mispronunciations resulting from imperfect recall of auditory patterns or defective auditory monitoring. These mispronunciations can be corrected easily by ear and tend to drop out early in the course of recovery. (Tests 3, 4, 5, 6, etc.)

5. Reduction of vocabulary evidenced by word-finding errors, disrupted communication, or circumlocutions. (Tests 7–15.)

Speech and Language Disturbances

6. Reduction of length and completeness of verbal units. Speech consists largely of disconnected words and phrases. This impairment correlates with reduction of vocabulary and verbal retention span throughout the course of recovery. (Tests 10, 11, 12, 15.)

7. Reduction of verbal retention span. Milder reduction of verbal retention span is reflected in the language behavior of subjects who forget what they were asked, what they have just said, or what they started to say. They frequently follow a tangential association, and lose the original intent completely. Speech tends to sound vague and incoherent. Such patients have sometimes been misdiagnosed as mentally confused, but behavior is reasonable and language performance good within limits of existing verbal span. (Tests 10, 14, 15.)

Test 1. Imitating Gross Movements of the Speech Musculature

Test 1 involves peripheral examination of the speech musculature. For the purpose of factor analysis, as well as differential diagnosis, tests related to each structure (larynx, tongue, palate, jaw, pharynx) were scored and coded separately. Test 1 and Test 2, rapid alternating movements, constituted Factor 4, the only factor related to movements that emerged on factor analysis. Varimax loadings [10] on tests included on Factor 4 were as follows:

```
Tongue movements  .....................  .72
Jaw movements  ........................  .71
Difficulty in swallowing  .................  .71
Phonation  ............................  .68
Palatal movements  .....................  .68
Rapid alternating movements  ............  .62
```

The inclusion of difficulty in swallowing on Factor 4 confirmed the hypothesis that Factor 4 represented dysarthria resulting from paralysis or weakness of the speech musculature.

Table 8 shows the intercorrelations between tests for gross movements of the speech musculature, and correlations of the same tests with four representative language tests. It can be readily observed that correlations between tests for gross movements are considerably higher than correlations between these tests and language tests, indicating that most of the variance in language performance must be

Differential Diagnosis of Aphasia

Table 8. Correlations between Gross Movements of the Speech Musculature, and between Gross Movements and Representative Language Tests

Test	Phonation	Tongue	Jaw	Palate	Pharynx
Gross Movements					
Phonation	..	.64	.54	.54	.53
Tongue	.64	..	.86	.59	.59
Jaw	.54	.86	..	.56	.54
Palate	.54	.59	.56	..	.59
Pharynx	.55	.59	.54	.59	..
Language Tests					
Naming pictures	.09	.49	.28	.28	.18
Definitions	.25	.64	.33	.39	.19
Picture description	.20	.55	.26	.41	.21
Similarities	.19	.54	.26	.27	.27

attributable to factors other than movement. The tests for tongue movements had the highest language loadings of tests for gross movements. These loadings are attributable at least in part to the former inclusion of items such as difficulty in initiating movements and rate of movements on Test 1, since these disabilities may reflect sensorimotor impairment rather than dysarthria. This has been corrected, so that Test 1 may now be regarded as a test for dysarthria. Nonaphasic subjects made no errors on Test 1.

The data in the tabulation indicate that only minimal impairment

PERFORMANCE ON GROSS MOVEMENTS OF SPEECH MUSCULATURE

Diagnostic Group	Number	Mean	Percentage of Subjects Making Errors
Simple	12	0.25	8
Visual	8	0.13	13
Persisting Dysfluency[a]	7	*1.00*	43
Scattered findings	26	0.96	50
Sensorimotor	11	0.09	9
Auditory (1)	6	0.00	0
Auditory (2)[a]	17	*0.82*	43
Irreversible	12	2.00	42
Total aphasic subjects	75	0.72 (SD = 1.86)	36
Total nonaphasic subjects ..	50	0.00	0

[a] Not included in the totals.

56

of gross movements was observed in the simple aphasia, visual, and sensorimotor groups. One patient in each group showed some reduction of rate or coordination of tongue movements. All limitations of extent of movement were in the scattered-findings and irreversible groups.

Test 2. Rapid Alternating Movements

Test 2 had its highest loadings on movement (.62) and language (.59) factors. Correlations above .70 were obtained with counting to 20 (.86), naming the days of the week (.79), repeating monosyllables (.76), repeating digits (.74), tongue movements (.72), and repeating sentences (.70).

Since it employs phonemes, Test 2 has a closer relationship with other language tests than Test 1. The rate of alternating movements may be impaired when paresis is present, or when there is poor sensory control of movement patterns. The diagnostic value of Test 2 depends upon the constellation of deficits present. When gross movements are defective, performance on Test 2 will reflect this impairment. When gross movements are normal, impaired performance on Test 2 usually reflects poor sensorimotor control. Nonaphasic subjects made no errors on Test 2.

Performance by diagnostic groups is summarized in the tabulation.

PERFORMANCE ON RAPID ALTERNATING
MOVEMENTS

Diagnostic Group	Number	Mean	Percentage of Subjects Making Errors
Simple	12	0.08	8
Visual	8	0.25	25
Persisting Dysfluency[a]	7	3.00	71
Scattered findings	26	1.40	65
Sensorimotor	11	1.45	73
Auditory (1)	6	1.83	50
Auditory (2)[a]	17	2.65	76
Irreversible	12	3.83	92
Total aphasic subjects	75	1.65 (SD = 2.26)	56
Total nonaphasic subjects	50	0.00	0

[a] Not included in the totals.

57

Differential Diagnosis of Aphasia

Test 3. Repeating Monosyllables

Words used on Test 3 are phonetically edited. Words were used rather than phonemes to elicit maximal performance from aphasic subjects [4]. Short words were used to minimize sequencing difficulties. The purpose of Test 3 is to assess the patient's ability to produce phonemes used in English. Sixty-one per cent of aphasic subjects made errors, compared with 4 per cent of nonaphasic subjects. Nonaphasic errors usually result from mishearing a word, absence of teeth, foreign accent, or occasionally a lifelong articulation defect. The fact that the nonaphasic population was screened for conditions that might be expected to reduce test validity, such as perceptual deficits, a history of neurological and psychiatric disease, and illiteracy, is probably responsible for the low percentage of articulation errors observed in nonaphasic subjects.

Test 3 had loadings of .84 and .34 on language and movement factors respectively. Correlations above .80 were obtained with defining words (.91), repeating digits (.90), naming the days of the week (.90), completing sentences (.89), describing a picture (.89), counting to 20 (.88), expressing ideas (.88), explaining similarities* (.88), oral spelling (.88), answering simple questions (.88), naming pictures (.87), repeating sentences (.86), giving biographical information (.82), writing a paragraph (.82), producing written sentences (.80). Thus repetition of monosyllabic words correlates more highly with language tests than with tests for gross movements of the speech musculature. The latter correlations were as follows: phonation (.41), tongue movements (.71), jaw movements (.47), palatal movements (.44), pharyngeal movements (.28), and rapid alternating movements (.76).

On factor analysis [10] the language loadings on three tests increased in inverse ratio to loadings on the movement factor, as follows:

	Language Factor	Movement Factor
Imitation of tongue movements....	.35	.72
Rapid alternating movements	.59	.62
Repetition of monosyllables	.82	.34

These findings appear to indicate that language tasks are more

58

dependent upon integrity of the learned code than upon intact musculature, which is not really surprising. Some degree of compensation is usually possible, and phonemes can vary over a considerable range without interfering with intelligibility of messages. The moot point is that ability to imitate gross movements of the speech musculature is not a sufficient condition to ensure normal articulation.

Clinical observation suggests the hypothesis that articulation is dependent upon both auditory and proprioceptive organization and control, as well as upon reasonable integrity of structure. This hypothesis permits the following interpretation of the findings in specific diagnostic groups (shown in the tabulation):

PERFORMANCE ON REPEATING MONOSYLLABLES

Diagnostic Group	Number	Mean	Percentage of Subjects Making Errors
Simple	12	1.00	17
Visual	8	1.00	13
Persisting Dysfluency[a]	7	6.57	71
Scattered findings	26	3.80	54
Sensorimotor	11	10.36	100
Auditory (1)	6	11.67	100
Auditory (2)[a]	17	17.12	88
Irreversible	12	24.75	100
Total aphasic subjects	75	8.00 (SD = 3.27)	61
Total nonaphasic subjects	50	0.08 (SD = 0.31)	4

[a] Not included in the totals.

Inconsistent mispronunciations occur in simple and visual aphasics as a result of imperfect auditory control.

Both auditory and proprioceptive discriminations are impaired in sensorimotor patients; hence the consistent character of the sensorimotor defect and the persistence of labored and nonfluent speech on all except short, highly overlearned utterances. Sensorimotor impairment is correlated with reduction of language at all stages of recovery.

In auditory patients, repetition is consistently more impaired than spontaneous speech. Jargon, sound substitutions, and struggle

Differential Diagnosis of Aphasia

behavior occur on both repetition and naming, but spontaneous verbal output increases rapidly, and sentences appear very early that sound completely normal. All the observed behavior indicates that the underlying problem is basically auditory. The language system appears to be relatively intact, but cut off from sensory input. Visual information is usually more effective than auditory in mediating output, but a combination of the two may be required initially to elicit a given response.

In scattered-findings aphasics, and frequently in irreversible patients, the musculature usually does not function effectively, and impaired articulation may result from a variety of causes, including partial paralysis of the palate or the tongue, or muscular weakness involving all speech structures. In irreversible patients sensorimotor impairment similar to that observed in sensorimotor patients is frequently found.

Test 4. Repeating Phrases

Sixty-seven per cent of aphasic and 4 per cent of nonaphasic subjects made errors on Test 4. Whereas Test 3 is a fairly simple test for production of phonemes, Test 4 makes it possible to observe disruptions of fluency and whether articulation tends to disintegrate in connected speech.

PERFORMANCE ON REPEATING PHRASES

Diagnostic Group	Number	Mean	Percentage of Subjects Making Errors
Simple	12	0.41	17
Visual	8	0.75	25
Persisting Dysfluency[a]	*7*	*3.14*	*71*
Scattered findings	26	3.30	61
Sensorimotor	11	9.90	100
Auditory (1)	6	14.33	100
Auditory (2)[a]	*17*	*16.35*	*88*
Irreversible	12	16.92	92
Total aphasic subjects	75	6.57 (SD = 7.61)	67
Total nonaphasic subjects	50	0.04 (SD = 0.20)	4

[a] Not included in the totals.

60

Speech and Language Disturbances

Performance of subjects by diagnostic categories is summarized in the tabulation.

Test 4 was not included on factor analysis.

Test 5. Counting to 20

Counting is one of the highly overlearned serial tasks that tends to run off automatically when the series is started. Subjects who cannot count to 20 upon direction frequently achieve partial success if the examiner supplies the first two or three numbers. Irreversible subjects can frequently count to 100 with practice. The task is chiefly useful for activating speech patterns and securing verbal responses from patients with severe aphasia.

Subjects with less severe impairment sometimes omit numbers, or break down somewhere in the middle of the series. They are frequently able to continue if the examiner supplies the next number.

Counting to 20 had its highest factor loadings on language (.77) and movement factors (.44). It correlated most highly with naming the days of the week (.94), oral spelling (.93), repeating digits (.91), repeating sentences (.90), rapid alternating movements (.86), repeating monosyllables (.86), completing sentences (.86), and giving biographical information (.85).

Forty per cent of aphasic and no nonaphasic subjects made errors in counting to 20. The mean error was 2.84, indicating that most

PERFORMANCE ON COUNTING TO 20

Diagnostic Group	Number	Mean	Percentage of Subjects Making Errors
Simple	21	0.00	0
Visual	27	0.63	11
Persisting Dysfluency*	7	0.00	0
Scattered findings	65	2.41	40
Sensorimotor	18	4.39	67
Auditory (1)	3	3.00	33
Auditory (2)*	17	7.41	88
Irreversible	23	8.00	96
Total aphasic subjects	157	2.84 (SD = 3.87)	40
Total nonaphasic subjects	100	0.00	0

* Not included in the totals.

61

Differential Diagnosis of Aphasia

subjects experienced partial success. However, coded scores (0–9) were used, so the means obtained underestimate total errors.

The tabulation shows the mean number of coded errors and the percentage of subjects by diagnostic categories who made errors on Test 5.

Test 6. Naming Days of Week

Forty-three per cent of aphasic and no nonaphasic subjects made errors in naming the days of the week. The correlation between counting to 20 and naming the days of the week was .94. As in counting, subjects who could not name the days of the week upon direction were sometimes able to complete the series when it was started by the examiner. Naming the days of the week had a higher factor loading on language (.86) than counting, and a somewhat lower loading (.32) on movements of the speech musculature.

Correlations above .85 were obtained with repeating digits (.95), counting to 20 (.94), oral spelling (.94), repeating sentences (.93), defining words (.92), naming pictures (.91), giving biographical information (.91), describing a picture (.91), repeating monosyllables (.90), expressing ideas (.90), answering simple questions (.89), completing sentences (.88), producing written sentences (.87), writing a paragraph (.86), oral reading (.86), and writing sentences to dictation.

PERFORMANCE ON NAMING DAYS OF WEEK

Diagnostic Group	Number	Mean	Percentage of Subjects Making Errors
Simple	21	0.00	0
Visual	27	0.26	49
Persisting Dysfluency[a]	*7*	*0.14*	*14*
Scattered findings	65	2.09	45
Sensorimotor	18	3.78	67
Auditory (1)	3	3.00	100
Auditory (2)[a]	*17*	*4.65*	*88*
Irreversible	23	6.48	96
Total aphasic subjects	157	2.35 (SD = 3.14)	43
Total nonaphasic subjects	100	0.00	0

[a] Not included in the totals.

62

Speech and Language Disturbances

Performance of subjects by diagnostic groups is summarized in the tabulation.

Test 7. Completing Sentences

Test 7 is the easiest of the language tests, if we define language tests as tests that involve meaningful use of language. The task is easy because given sentences provide frames in which the response to be elicited has a high probability of occurrence. Such elicited responses are similar to the reactive speech of aphasic subjects described by Weisenburg and McBride [12]. They also resemble popular responses elicited from normal subjects on word-association tests. Associated responses indicate that some of the underlying structure of language is intact, but they do not constitute voluntary speech, nor do they necessarily indicate that voluntary speech will be recovered.

Forty-three per cent of aphasic subjects made errors in sentence completion, while nonaphasic subjects made no errors.

Sentence completion had a loading of .93 on the language factor on factor analysis; there were no other significant factor loadings. It correlated most highly with Test 8 (.97), answering simple questions. Correlations above .90 were obtained with repeating sentences (.94), naming pictures (.94), repeating digits (.94), giving biographical information (.93), describing a picture (.93), repeating

PERFORMANCE ON COMPLETING SENTENCES

Diagnostic Group	Number	Mean	Percentage of Subjects Making Errors
Simple	12	0.08	8
Visual	8	0.13	13
Persisting Dysfluency [a]	*7*	*0.14*	*14*
Scattered findings	26	0.46	23
Sensorimotor	11	2.09	64
Auditory (1)	6	4.83	86
Auditory (2) [a]	*17*	*5.53*	*88*
Irreversible	12	5.83	100
Total aphasic subjects	75	1.81 (SD = 2.83)	43
Total nonaphasic subjects ..	50	0.00	0

[a] Not included in the totals.

Differential Diagnosis of Aphasia

monosyllables (.91), defining words (.90), and expressing ideas (.90).

Performance by diagnostic categories is summarized in the tabulation.

Test 8. Answering Simple Questions

Answering simple questions requires a one-word response to a short question that supplies a high-strength association with the word to be elicited. Responding to a question is usually a little more difficult for aphasic subjects than completing a sentence, which, in Chomsky's terminology [2], requires no transformation of sentence form. As a result the stimulus is more immediate.

PERFORMANCE ON ANSWERING SIMPLE QUESTIONS

Diagnostic Group	Number	Mean	Percentage of Subjects Making Errors
Simple	12	0.17	17
Visual	8	0.13	13
Persisting Dysfluency a	7	0.57	29
Scattered findings	26	0.85	27
Sensorimotor	11	3.82	82
Auditory (1)	6	5.50	100
Auditory (2) a	17	6.65	100
Irreversible	12	7.75	100
Total aphasic subjects	75	2.57 (SD = 3.31)	49
Total nonaphasic subjects ..	50	0.00	0

ᵃ Not included in the totals.

A patient who cannot produce the word *chair* when naming pictures frequently responds correctly if asked what you sit in. Similarly a patient who cannot answer the question may supply the word *chair* in response to the frame "You sit in a ——." The patient who is beginning to be able to answer simple questions appears to have taken the first step toward voluntary speech. When he can name objects without such assistance speech usually begins to be functional.

Forty-nine per cent of aphasic and no nonaphasic subjects made errors in responding to simple questions.

Test 8 had a factor loading of .96 on language and no other significant loadings. The loading on Factor 4, concerned with movements of the speech musculature, was .07.

Correlations above .85 were obtained with completing sentences (.97), defining words (.94), giving biographical information (.94), naming pictures (.93), describing a picture (.93), expressing ideas (.92), repeating digits (.91), naming the days of the week (.89), and oral spelling (.89).

Performance by diagnostic groups is summarized in the tabulation.

Test 9. Giving Biographical Information

Test 9 requires subjects to give common but accurate biographical information and some elaboration of responses. Sixty-four per cent of aphasic and no nonaphasic subjects failed to respond adequately.

Test 9 had a factor loading of .91 on language and no other significant factor loadings. Correlations above .85 were obtained with describing a picture (.97), answering simple questions (.94), completing sentences (.93), naming pictures (.93), defining words (.93), expressing ideas (.93), repeating sentences (.91), repeating digits (.91), naming the days of the week (.91), following directions (.88), oral spelling (.86), identifying objects named serially (.85), and counting to 20 (.85).

PERFORMANCE ON GIVING BIOGRAPHICAL
INFORMATION

Diagnostic Group	Number	Mean	Percentage of Subjects Making Errors
Simple	12	0.50	17
Visual	8	0.75	38
Persisting Dysfluency [a]	7	4.14	43
Scattered findings	26	3.04	58
Sensorimotor	11	9.18	100
Auditory (1)	6	9.33	83
Auditory (2) [a]	17	11.59	100
Irreversible	12	14.50	100
Total aphasic subjects	75	5.63 (SD = 6.10)	64
Total nonaphasic subjects	50	0.00	0

[a] Not included in the totals.

Differential Diagnosis of Aphasia

Performance of subjects by diagnostic categories is summarized in the tabulation.

Test 10. Expressing Ideas

This test requires the subject to tell three things he has done during the day and three things a good citizen should do. Although expressing ideas correlates highly with giving biographical information, the test was retained because it enables the examiner to observe if the patient is able to remember instructions long enough to complete an utterance of several parts, and if he has enough functional language to deal with ideas that are relatively impersonal and a little re-

PERFORMANCE ON EXPRESSING IDEAS

Diagnostic Group	Number	Mean	Percentage of Subjects Making Errors
Simple	12	0.33	25
Visual	8	0.38	25
Persisting Dysfluency [a]	7	1.43	43
Scattered findings	26	1.19	58
Sensorimotor	11	4.36	100
Auditory (1)	6	3.50	100
Auditory (2) [a]	17	5.06	100
Irreversible	12	5.92	100
Total aphasic subjects	75	2.37 (SD = 2.39)	65
Total nonaphasic subjects	50	0.02 (SD = 0.14)	2

[a] Not included in the totals.

mote from the immediate situation. Sixty-five per cent of aphasic subjects failed to complete the task, and one out of 50 nonaphasic subjects was unable to think of a third thing a good citizen should do.

Expressing ideas had a factor loading of .90 on language and no other significant factor loadings.

Correlations above .85 were obtained with defining words (.94), giving biographical information (.93), oral spelling (.93), answering simple questions (.92), naming pictures (.92), repeating sentences (.91), repeating digits (.91), completing sentences (.90),

Speech and Language Disturbances

naming the days of the week (.90), describing a picture (.90), repeating monosyllables (.88), and writing a paragraph (.85). Performance by diagnostic groups is summarized in the tabulation.

Test 11. Producing Sentences

Producing sentences requires the subject to give structurally correct sentences using words of various grammatical classes. Sixtyeight per cent of aphasic and no nonaphasic subjects made errors on this test. There was almost no performance in sensorimotor, auditory, or irreversible patients, although sensorimotor patients produced appropriate phrases and an occasional complete sentence, as did six patients in the auditory group. No irreversible subject produced any correct responses. Performance by diagnostic categories is summarized in the tabulation.

PERFORMANCE ON PRODUCING SENTENCES

Diagnostic Group	Number	Mean	Percentage of Subjects Making Errors
Simple	12	0.50	17
Visual	8	1.38	50
Persisting Dysfluency [a]	7	1.86	57
Scattered findings	26	1.85	62
Sensorimotor	11	5.27	100
Auditory (1)	6	5.50	100
Auditory (2) [a]	17	5.47	100
Irreversible	12	6.00	100
Total aphasic subjects	75	3.04 (SD = 2.68)	68
Total nonaphasic subjects	50	0.00	0

[a] Not included in the totals.

Test 12. Describing Picture

Picture description is a useful test for eliciting maximal language from patients with moderately severe aphasia. It enables the examiner to observe word-finding difficulty, fluency, length and completeness of utterances, and ability to integrate the multiple stimuli presented by the picture into meaningful statements.

Picture description had a factor loading of .93 on language and no other significant factor loadings. Correlations above .90 were ob-

Differential Diagnosis of Aphasia

tained with naming pictures (.97), giving biographical information (.97), completing sentences (.93), answering simple questions (.93), defining words (.92), naming the days of the week (.91), repeating digits (.91), and expressing ideas (.90).

PERFORMANCE ON DESCRIBING PICTURE

Diagnostic Group	Number	Mean	Percentage of Subjects Making Errors
Simple	12	1.00	50
Visual	8	1.50	75
Persisting Dysfluency [a]	7	2.14	86
Scattered findings	26	2.46	85
Sensorimotor	11	4.36	100
Auditory (1)	6	4.50	100
Auditory (2) [a]	17	5.47	100
Irreversible	12	6.00	100
Total aphasic subjects	75	3.16 (SD = 2.13)	84
Total nonaphasic subjects	50	0.00	0

[a] Not included in the totals.

Performance by diagnostic categories is summarized below. In general, persisting dysfluency and single aphasia subjects tended to make minor word-finding errors. They talked in sentences, although these broke down upon occasion. The performance of sensorimotor subjects consisted chiefly of naming, although short connected language units appeared. Both approximations of words and association errors were present. Patients with scattered findings tended to show word-finding errors together with dysarthria of various degrees. There was no performance for irreversible subjects.

Patients with intermittent auditory imperception usually made extremely defective responses when they were trying to name particular objects, but many of them also produced some sentences with normal articulation, inflection, and fluency. Sentence content tended to be vague and was sometimes incoherent, as in the following example:

Oh, heavens. Well, there was a little ice [kite]. Okay and okay [pointing to door and windows]. Here gramples [shrubbery]. Things to house [pointing to house] and three cans [sidewalk] and okay [mailbox]. S-u-n [attempting to read *Smith*, name on mailbox]. That's all. Okay what you will see for it.

Test 13. Naming Pictures

The first five words on Test 13 occur among the thousand most commonly used words in the English language, words 6–10 among the second thousand, words 11–15 among the third to the fifth thousand, and words 16–20 among the fifth through the tenth thousand, as listed by Thorndike and Lorge [11]. It was not feasible to include less common words than this on a test that used pictures, since few words of lower frequency can be represented in a manner that elicits a uniform response from nonaphasic subjects. Eighty-five per cent of aphasic and no nonaphasic subjects made errors in naming pictures.

Mean errors and percentages of errors for each of the four frequency lists for 75 aphasic subjects are shown below. Although differences between the four lists were small, the direction of differences, that is, the tendency for errors to increase as word frequency decreased, was consistent and in agreement with the findings of other studies of vocabulary in aphasia. The largest difference was between List 3 and List 4.

Word Frequency	Mean	Percentage of Total Errors
List 1 (first thousand words)	1.64	19
List 2 (second thousand words)..	1.91	23
List 3 (third through fifth thousand words)	2.16	26
List 4 (fifth through tenth thousand words)	2.75	32
Total	8.45	100

Word-finding errors were classified as follows: no response, 50 per cent; irrelevant response, 12 per cent; perseveration of a previous response, 3 per cent; approximation of correct word, 10 per cent; associated response, 25 per cent. No response was the most frequent type of error produced by subjects who made the most total errors, but it also occurred in subjects with good over-all performance. Whereas subjects with the largest error scores were usually unable to produce any response, subjects who made minimal errors sometimes

Differential Diagnosis of Aphasia

either named the picture accurately or said they did not know, apparently inhibiting incorrect responses.

Forty-eight per cent of errors in the simple aphasia group, 55 per cent in visual patients, and 51 per cent in the scattered-findings group, were association errors. Ninety per cent of errors in irreversible and 42 per cent of errors in sensorimotor patients consisted of no response. In general it is more meaningful to study changes in error types over time than over subjects. Thus one subject in the auditory group produced first a preponderance of jargon responses, next recognizable approximations of words (*soffee* for *coffee*, *cuppie* for *cup*) intermixed with perseveration of previous words, and finally associated words and correct responses began to appear.

The present test for naming objects is a revision of the test used on the factor analysis study, which was limited to the most commonly used words in the language. Since this would not be expected to change what the test measures, these data are probably still applicable. Naming common objects had a factor loading of .91 on language, and no other significant factor loadings. Correlations of .90 or above were obtained with describing a picture (.97), completing sentences (.94), defining words (.94), repeating digits (.93), answering simple questions (.93), giving biographical information (.93), expressing ideas (.92), naming the days of the week (.91), repeating sentences (.90), and oral reading (.90).

PERFORMANCE ON NAMING PICTURES

Diagnostic Group	Number	Mean	Percentage of Subjects Making Errors
Simple	12	1.92	58
Visual	8	5.25	100
Persisting Dysfluency [a]	7	2.57	57
Scattered findings	26	5.08	77
Sensorimotor	11	10.91	100
Auditory (1)	6	13.17	100
Auditory (2) [a]	17	15.82	100
Irreversible	12	19.83	100
Total aphasic subjects	75	8.45 (SD = 7.62)	85
Total nonaphasic subjects	50	0.00	0

[a] Not included in the totals.

70

Mean errors and percentages of subjects making errors on the revised test are shown in the tabulation. The discrepancy between simple and visual aphasics' scores on language tests has not been found in other studies. It can probably be accounted for by the small number of subjects in both groups, and particularly in the visual group.

Test 14. Defining Words

On most vocabulary tests the object is to determine if the patient knows the word, since the item is scored correct if the patient shows, even by a gesture, that he understands the meaning of the word. This is not true of the present test.

On Test 14, words were chosen that are familiar to most adults of average intelligence and average educational level. The only word not included among the first thousand most commonly used words in the English language [11] is *robin*. Robin is the "easiest" word to define in the series, since it readily elicits the popular association *bird*. The object of the present test is to determine if the subject has enough language to explain what a word means, or to say the same thing another way.

When the test was constructed, a list of 30 words was made up from commonly used words and administered to a series of aphasic and nonaphasic subjects. Words nonaphasic subjects had consistent difficulty defining were eliminated first. Next responses of aphasic patients were tabulated and analyzed. In general they fell into these classes: (1) correct explanation; (2) correct association or example; (3) vague repetition with no added information; (4) no meaningful response, or erroneous response. Words were then selected that produced the most differentiated responses from aphasic subjects, and scoring criteria were established on the basis of the obtained responses. Eighty-nine per cent of aphasic and 32 per cent of nonaphasic subjects made errors in defining words, with means of 6.08 (SD = 3.66) and 0.60 (SD = 1.07) respectively.

Defining words had a factor loading of .89 on language; there were no other significant factor loadings. Correlations of .90 or above were obtained with answering simple questions (.94), naming pictures

Differential Diagnosis of Aphasia

(.94), expressing ideas (.94), giving biographical information (.93), repeating digits (.92), naming the days of the week (.92), describing a picture (.92), repeating monosyllables (.91), oral spelling (.91), repeating sentences (.90), completing sentences (.90), and producing written sentences (.90).

PERFORMANCE ON DEFINING WORDS

Diagnostic Group	Number	Mean	Percentage of Subjects Making Errors
Simple	12	2.25	58
Visual	8	4.25	88
Persisting Dysfluency [a]	7	3.43	86
Scattered findings	26	4.96	92
Sensorimotor	11	8.36	100
Auditory (1)	6	9.17	100
Auditory (2) [a]	17	9.76	100
Irreversible	12	9.92	100
Total aphasic subjects	75	6.08 (SD = 3.66)	89
Total nonaphasic subjects	50	0.60 (SD = 1.07)	32

[a] Not included in the totals.

Performance by diagnostic groups is summarized in the tabulation. In general subjects in simple aphasia, visual, and persisting dysfluency groups were able to define most words, or produce reasonably good examples. Subjects in the sensorimotor group were sometimes able to say *bird* for *robin* or even *fruit* for *apple*, but for the most part tended to produce associated responses such as *bridge: cross the bridge*, or *decide: decide to go*. In the irreversible and auditory groups virtually no meaningful responses occurred.

Test 15. Retelling Paragraph

Retelling a paragraph has been substituted for explaining proverbs, which was used on earlier test forms, because retelling a paragraph had a higher test ceiling; because the factor structure of explaining proverbs (.79 on language, .45 on stimulus equivalence) made for uncertainty as to what the test was measuring; and because responses of nonaphasic subjects frequently tended to be equivocal.

It also seems probable that some proverbs are more familiar to some cultural subgroups than to others.

Ninety-nine per cent of aphasic subjects and 28 per cent of non-aphasic subjects made errors in retelling a paragraph, with means of 4.59 (SD = 1.63) and 0.74 (SD = 1.31) respectively.

In general the errors of nonaphasic subjects reflected poor memory in some of the older patients. These subjects tended to reminisce at length about relevant personal experiences or previous information, somewhat in the manner of college students inadequately prepared for an examination. The responses of aphasic subjects, on the other hand, tended to be more constricted than expansive. Some mild aphasic subjects made irrelevant responses, but these tended to be vague and incoherent rather than related to personal experiences or previous information.

TESTS ELIMINATED

Besides explaining proverbs two other tests, producing rhyming words and explaining similarities, which were included in the factor analysis [10] have been eliminated from this section of the test. Since these are good tests some discussion is in order.

It was observed very early that few aphasic patients, and in general only those with minimal or mild aphasia, could rhyme. Subjects consistently made no response or produced words associated with the given word by meaning rather than by sound, as *car* and *drive* or *tree* and *bark*. Test directions were revised to use the phrase *a word that sounds like* as well as *a word that rhymes,* and generous examples were given, without affecting test results significantly. Biondo in an unpublished study observed a similar difficulty in producing rhymes among children in a state school for the deaf.

Rhyming had a factor loading of .84 on language, and no other significant loadings. It correlated highly with all other language tests.

Seventy-nine per cent of aphasic and 14 per cent of nonaphasic subjects made errors in producing rhyming words, with means of 2.77 (SD = 5.76) and 0.32 (SD = 0.93) respectively. Two out of 50 nonaphasic subjects could produce no rhymes at all.

An interesting observation was that aphasic subjects with partial

73

auditory imperception frequently produced rhyming words inadvertently when attempting to name pictures. Thus a patient who could produce no rhymes voluntarily called a cow a *how*, a *pow*, and a *tow* successively. He did not say *cow* at all, although he had no difficulty producing the *k* sound, as evinced by the fact that he named *cup* and *comb* correctly on the same task. The explanation is that the patient was not rhyming when he said *how, pow, tow,* but groping for an auditory pattern he recalled only in part. Inability to rhyme, on the other hand, reflects inability to match by sound. Thus both kind of errors reflect impairment of auditory processes, and one should expect them to occur together with some frequency.

It has been observed that some patients with whom work was being done to re-establish phonemic discrimination as a basis for reading and writing have depended on visual rather than auditory cues, and have been betrayed by writing *shave, save, have,* or *bead, read, head* when asked to write words that sounded like a given word.

It is possible that the inability of nonaphasics to rhyme represents the lower end of a continuum, the upper end of which is probably represented by the sensitivity of poets to the sound of words, and which is analogous to the range between individuals who are tone-deaf and those who have perfect pitch. Rhyming was eliminated in the Minnesota Test partly because nonaphasic subjects were found who could not rhyme, but mostly because it seemed to contribute little to the range of language tests. It is a good supplementary test to use, however, when more exploration is desired.

Explaining similarities was also missed by 79 per cent of aphasic and 14 per cent of nonaphasic subjects, with means of 3.63 (SD = 2.98) and 0.16 (SD = 0.42) respectively. It had a factor loading of .91 on language, with no other significant loadings. Correlations above .90 were obtained with repeating digits, completing sentences, naming the days of the week, answering simple questions, naming pictures, rhyming,* defining words, giving biographical information, expressing ideas, and explaining proverbs.*

Patients with limited language tended to be able to deal with only one item at a time and to produce only a common association to each one. This resulted in responses such as *car: drive* and *airplane: fly*;

green: *go* and *red*: *stop*; or *go east*: *go west*, accompanied by pointing in opposite directions. On retest, when more language was available, the same patients frequently produced responses like *transportation, colors*, and *directions*.

Some nonaphasic subjects in older age groups, however, said flatly that the two items named were not alike, and proceeded to expound at length on differences, and why the differences were important.

Like rhyming, telling how two things are alike is still a good language test for aphasics, taxing vocabulary as it does. It was omitted chiefly because of overlap with other language tests.

5

Visuomotor and Writing Disturbances

Writing requires language and, in addition, learned visuomotor integrations. The writing of an aphasic patient often reflects reduction of language and nothing more.

The spelling of aphasic patients is usually disrupted to some degree. Letters have names, and aphasic patients have trouble discriminating names of letters that sound alike, names associated by position in the alphabet, and names of letters used least frequently in English. With reduced verbal retention span, aphasic subjects also have difficulty in recalling and ordering the sequences of letters that constitute words. Bricker, Schuell, and Jenkins [1] found that spelling errors of aphasic subjects can be accounted for almost entirely by word frequency and word length. In other words, aphasic populations make fewer errors in writing common words than words that are more uncommon in the language, and in general make fewer errors in writing short words than long ones.

Most aphasic patients tend to write the way they talk. Word-finding errors occur in written as in spoken language. Patients who have difficulty talking in sentences have difficulty writing sentences. If connected speech tends to be vague and incoherent, written language is vague and incoherent, too. Writing usually tends to be a little more impaired than speaking, although discrepancies are not great unless there is additional impairment affecting writing and not speech.

Visuomotor and Writing Disturbances

There appear to be two kinds of impairment with this effect. The first is impaired discrimination and recall of letter forms. The second is disturbance of spatial perception characterized by confusion of directionality and distorted perception of spatial relationships.

Both of these dimensions appeared on factor analysis. Factor 2, which included tests for discrimination of visual forms and recognition and recall of learned visual symbols, had a correlation of .61 with Factor 1, which was the language factor, and a correlation of .55 with Factor 3, the visuospatial factor. Factor 3 also had a correlation of .58 with Factor 4, which involved gross movements of the speech musculature. Concerning the interesting intercorrelations of factors, Schuell, Jenkins, and Carroll [10] observed: "On the present analysis Factor 1, language behavior, was most highly correlated with Factor 2, visual discrimination (on matching, recognition, and recall). It was not identical with it, however, since not all language behavior involves visual discrimination. Factor 2 was also highly intercorrelated with Factor 3, visuospatial behavior, but not identical with it, since Factor 3 required proprioceptive as well as visual information. Factor 3 was most highly intercorrelated with Factor 4, gross movements of the speech musculature on which proprioceptive processes also were represented to some extent."

The problem of differential diagnosis of writing impairment is to determine if the performance of an aphasic patient reflects reduction of language, impaired visual recall, spatial imperception, or some combination of these dimensions.

Aphasic patients with impaired visual discrimination usually show impaired recall of letter forms. When the disability is severe the patient cannot write any letters or words. He must relearn the alphabet letter by letter, upper case, lower case, print and script. Patients with milder impairment tend to confuse letters with similar visual configurations. Such a patient might spell *week* correctly aloud, but write *MFFk*. Contrary to popular belief printing is initially easier than script for patients with severe impairment of visual recall, perhaps because the problem of connecting letters does not arise. These patients frequently use proprioceptive cues to aid defective visual information, tracing a letter on a page or in the air before attempting to name or write it. When letter forms are relearned, handwriting becomes normal.

Many aphasic patients cannot write with the preferred hand because it is paralyzed. They usually transfer readily to the other hand with a little practice. There is some initial clumsiness and occasional reversals occur, but these are transient phenomena, and often marked proficiency is attained. Occasionally, however, an aphasic patient shows persisting impairment of fine movements in the nonparalyzed hand, which extends to tasks other than writing. Impaired control of hand movements is usually characterized by confusion of directionality. On copying letters, for example, the patient often appears not to know where to start the letter, or in which direction to proceed. He does not know whether to go up or down, or right or left, and may confuse directions in the middle of a letter, producing distortions of letter forms. These patients are often critical of results, and may sketch in lines to improve the appearance of a letter, showing ability to utilize visual information.

With severe spatial disorientation patients are unable to copy even simple forms, and writing is rarely recovered.

SUPPLEMENTARY TESTS

Of supplementary tests, the Jastak and Bijou *Wide Range Achievement Test* is useful because it provides an estimate of spelling vocabulary that can be compared with educational level, and because it is sensitive to increments that occur with recovery of language.

The Goodenough draw-a-man test often reveals spatial disorientation and sometimes specific impairment of body image as well. It is not uncommon for patients with severe reduction of sensation on one side of the body to omit this side from the drawing. One patient who had drawn a head supported by half a figure was pressed to draw the other leg. He was reluctant, but finally added it as a perpendicular appendage to the foot he had already drawn.

There is such a wide range in drawings of non-brain-injured adults, particularly in older age groups, that it is generally unwise to attach any significance to errors other than gross distortions of spatial relationships. Both the *Bender Visual Motor Gestalt Test* and the *Ben-*

78

ton Revised Visual Retention Test are useful tests, however, for demonstrating such deficits. The Benton Test has the added advantage of containing peripheral figures that may be useful in indicating hemianopsia. One should be cautious in diagnosing poor visual recall on the basis of recall of figures, however, since what the aphasic patient may not be able to do is to tell himself that one card contained a row of dots or two interlinked circles with a small square at the periphery. In other words, nonlanguage tests may be mediated by language to some unknown extent.

Object assembly tests are also useful for exploring visuospatial disorders. The manikin and the profile from the *Wechsler Adult Intelligence Scale* were included on the factor analysis. Both tests obtained their highest factor loadings (.66) on visuospatial behavior.

TESTS INCLUDED IN SECTION D OF THE MINNESOTA TEST

The first five tests in Section D (Visuomotor and Writing Disturbances) involve the ability to reproduce or recall visual forms, while the last five deal more specifically with written language. These dimensions are not mutually exclusive, however, as factorial structures show.

Upon completion of Section D the examiner should be able to discriminate between reduction of writing secondary to reduction of language, impaired discrimination and recall of letter forms, impaired spatial perception, and some combination of these. (When spatial perception is impaired, impairment of body image should be investigated.) The examiner should also be able to evaluate the extent to which the following factors disturb writing performance:

1. Impaired visuospatial perception (Tests 1, 3, 4).
2. Impaired visual recall (Tests 2, 5, 6).
3. Reduction of language (Tests 7, 8, 9, 10).

Performance of aphasic and nonaphasic subjects on Section D is summarized in Table 9.

Test 1. Copying Greek Letters

Copying Greek letters is a relatively easy copying task. It enables the examiner to observe whether the patient has difficulty holding or

Differential Diagnosis of Aphasia

Table 9. Tests for Visuomotor and Writing Impairment: Means, Standard Deviations, Median Scores, and Percentage of Subjects Making Errors

Test	No.	Mean	SD	Median	Percentage of Subjects Making Errors
1. Copying Greek letters					
Aphasics	75	0.49	1.27	0	21
Nonaphasics	50	0.02	0.14	0	2
2. Writing numbers to 20					
Aphasics	75	2.29	5.54	0	27
Nonaphasics	50	0.00	0.00	0	0
3. Reproducing wheel					
Aphasics	75	0.75	1.33	0	36
Nonaphasics	50	0.16	0.47	0	2
4. Reproducing letters					
Aphasics	75	2.65	4.04	1	67
Nonaphasics	50	0.02	0.14	0	2
5. Writing letters to dictation					
Aphasics	75	7.73	9.08	4	75
Nonaphasics	50	0.08	0.27	0	8
6. Written spelling					
Aphasics	75	6.08	4.09	8	81
Nonaphasics	50	0.76	1.56	0	36
7. Oral spelling					
Aphasics	75	6.28	4.19	9	81
Nonaphasics	50	0.62	1.46	0	26
8. Producing written sentences					
Aphasics	75	4.53	5.01	6	89
Nonaphasics	50	0.52	0.93	0	34
9. Writing sentences to dictation					
Aphasics	75	5.43	2.29	8	96
Nonaphasics	50	0.80	0.64	0	38
10. Writing a paragraph					
Aphasics	75	4.64	1.95	6	95
Nonaphasics	50	0.26	0.72	0	14

guiding a pencil, faulty eye-hand coordination, or confused directionality reflecting defective perception of spatial relationships. The figures are too gross, however, to reveal mild impairment of visual discrimination.

Test 1 had a loading of .89 on visuospatial perception, with no other significant factor loadings. Correlations above .70 were obtained with matching pictures* (.90), reproducing letters (.89), copying forms* (.77), matching forms (.76), drawing a house* (.76), reproducing a wheel (.75), drawing a man* (.71), and matching words to pictures (.70). The high correlations between copying and matching tests refute the hypothesis that impaired copying is primarily a defect of execution.

PERFORMANCE ON COPYING GREEK LETTERS

Diagnostic Group	Number	Mean	Percentage of Subjects Making Errors
Simple	12	0.00	0
Visual	8	0.13	13
Persisting Dysfluency [a]	*7*	*0.00*	*0*
Scattered findings	26	0.50	23
Sensorimotor	11	0.09	9
Auditory (1)	6	0.00	0
Auditory (2) [a]	*17*	*0.41*	*18*
Irreversible	12	1.83	67
Total aphasic subjects	75	0.49 (SD = 1.27)	21
Total nonaphasic subjects..	50	0.02 (SD = 0.14)	2

[a] Not included in the totals.

Nonaphasic subjects made minimal errors in copying Greek letters, and most aphasic subjects were able to perform the task adequately using the non-preferred hand when the preferred hand was paralyzed. The tabulation summarizes the performance of subjects in various diagnostic categories.

Test 2. Writing Numbers to 20

Twenty-seven per cent of aphasic and no nonaphasic patients made errors in writing numbers from 1 to 20. While Test 2 is less pure than Test 1 from a factorial standpoint, this merely demonstrates that more than one dimension must be taken into account in assessing writing impairment in aphasia, even on relatively simple tasks. Writing numbers from 1 to 20 had a factor loading of .56 on visual discrimination, recognition, and recall; of .46 on spatial perception; and of .33 on language.

The factorial structure was reflected in clinical performances.

Differential Diagnosis of Aphasia

There were subjects who omitted numbers in the series and subjects who got as far as 6 or 7, or 11 or 12, and could go no farther. There were subjects who could not remember what an 8 or 9 looked like, and subjects who reversed 3's and 4's and confused 6's and 9's.

Correlations above .70 were obtained with matching pictures* (.88), writing sentences to dictation (.79), setting a clock (.78), written spelling (.76), writing a paragraph (.74), solving simple stated problems* (.74), writing letters to dictation (.73), writing words to auditory* (.71) and to visual stimulation* (.70), producing written sentences (.71), long division (.71), and drawing a house* (.70).

Performance by diagnostic groups is summarized in the tabulation.

PERFORMANCE ON WRITING NUMBERS TO 20

Diagnostic Group	Number	Mean	Percentage of Subjects Making Errors
Simple	12	0.00	0
Visual	8	0.63	13
Persisting Dysfluency [a]	7	*0.75*	*16*
Scattered findings	26	1.85	27
Sensorimotor	11	0.45	8
Auditory (1)	6	0.00	0
Auditory (2) [a]	*17*	*5.76*	*47*
Irreversible	12	9.50	92
Total aphasic subjects	75	2.29 (SD = 5.54)	27
Total nonaphasic subjects	50	0.00	0

[a] Not included in the totals.

Test 3. Reproducing Wheel

Reproducing a wheel is presumably a little more difficult than copying Greek letters because the stimulus is withdrawn before the task is executed and the subject is forced to depend upon visual memory. Reproducing a wheel is primarily a test of spatial perception, however, since a wheel is a common object, and the figure is scored correct if the subject produces a recognizable circle, with spokes that approximate the rim in all quadrants and intersect in the general area of the center of the circle. Subjects with spatial disorientation sometimes draw parallel spokes running horizontally or

82

vertically, or sometimes spokes attached to a segment of a radius in a constricted sector.

Reproducing a wheel had a factor loading of .70 on visuospatial perception and .28 on visual discrimination, recognition, and recall. The latter loading is probably not significant. Correlations above .65 were obtained with matching letters (.86), copying Greek letters (.75), drawing a man (.69), reproducing letters (.67), counting to 20 (.67), matching forms (.65), and simple numerical combinations (.65). Errors by diagnostic categories are shown below.

PERFORMANCE ON REPRODUCING WHEEL

Diagnostic Group	Number	Mean	Percentage of Subjects Making Errors
Simple	12	0.08	8
Visual	8	0.13	13
Persisting Dysfluency [a]	*7*	*0.42*	*14*
Scattered findings	26	0.73	42
Sensorimotor	11	0.27	27
Auditory (1)	6	1.33	50
Auditory (2) [a]	*17*	*1.24*	*43*
Irreversible	12	2.00	67
Total aphasic subjects	75	0.75 (SD = 1.33)	36
Total nonaphasic subjects	50	0.16 (SD = 0.47)	12

[a] Not included in the totals.

Test 4. Reproducing Letters

Significant errors on Test 4 are those that involve reversals or distortions of letter forms. Occasional confusions between upper- and lower-case forms usually appeared to result from carelessness in following instructions. Reproducing letters had a factor loading of .70 on visuospatial perception and .32 on visual discrimination, recognition, and recall.

Correlations above .70 were obtained with reproducing Greek letters (.86), matching pictures* (.86), drawing a house* (.79), matching forms (.75), reading comprehension, short paragraph* (.74), multiplication (.74), reading rate (.72), writing words to visual stimulation* (.72), and producing written sentences (.71).

83

Differential Diagnosis of Aphasia

Performance by diagnostic groups is summarized in the tabulation.

PERFORMANCE ON REPRODUCING LETTERS

Diagnostic Group	Number	Mean	Percentage of Subjects Making Errors
Simple	12	0.42	33
Visual	8	1.25	50
Persisting Dysfluency [a]	*7*	*0.42*	*14*
Scattered findings.........	26	2.81	81
Sensorimotor	11	1.18	54
Auditory (1)	6	2.17	67
Auditory (2) [a]	*17*	*4.65*	*88*
Irreversible	12	7.08	92
Total aphasic subjects	75	2.65 (SD = 4.04)	67
Total nonaphasic subjects..	50	0.02 (SD = 0.14)	2

[a] Not included in the totals.

Test 5. Writing Letters to Dictation

Writing letters dictated in random order had a factor loading of .73 on visual discrimination, recognition, and recall; of .49 on language; and .31 on spatial perception. The factorial structure reminds us that we are dealing with learned visual patterns that have been integrated into the language system.

As on writing numbers, clinical performances reflected the dimensions that appeared on factor analysis. The most common errors were confusion between letters whose names sound alike, confusion between letters associated by serial position, and letters that occur comparatively rarely in English. Other subjects confused letters that look alike, or produced a preponderance of reversals and distortions of letter forms.

Correlations above .85 were obtained with written spelling (.95), writing words to auditory* (.94) and to visual stimulation* (.87), writing sentences to dictation (.94), pointing to letters named in random order (.91), matching printed to spoken words (.86), solving simple stated problems* (.86), writing a paragraph (.84), following directions (.83), oral reading, sentences (.82), and reading comprehension, paragraph (.81).

84

PERFORMANCE ON WRITING LETTERS TO DICTATION

Diagnostic Group	Number	Mean	Percentage of Subjects Making Errors
Simple	12	0.50	42
Visual	8	2.75	63
Persisting Dysfluency [a]	7	0.00	0
Scattered findings	26	5.81	73
Sensorimotor	11	5.91	91
Auditory (1)	6	12.67	83
Auditory (2) [a]	17	15.29	100
Irreversible	12	21.67	100
Total aphasic subjects	75	7.73 (SD = 9.08)	75
Total nonaphasic subjects	50	0.08 (SD = 0.27)	8

[a] Not included in the totals.

Performance by diagnostic groups is summarized in the tabulation.

Test 6. Written Spelling

Eighty-one per cent of aphasic and 36 per cent of nonaphasic subjects made errors on the test for written spelling, with means of 6.08 (SD = 4.09) and 0.76 (SD = 1.56) respectively. There is, of course, always an overlap between spelling and educational level, which necessitates qualitative judgments in interpreting test scores. The same score could be interpreted as compatible with educational and vocational level in one subject and as indicative of marked impairment in another. In addition, there are individuals of marked intellectual achievement who never attain any spelling proficiency, whether through inability to learn to spell or ineffective teaching methods. Sometimes the examiner can obtain a sample of the patient's previous writing for comparison, or if not, some information about previous writing habits from an informant or from the patient himself.

Words were selected from grade levels three through six on graded spelling lists, and an effort was made to avoid words frequently misspelled or confused by nonaphasic subjects.

Written spelling had a factor loading of .75 on visual discrimination, recognition, and recall, and .54 on language. Correlations above .85 were obtained with producing written sentences (.98), writing words to auditory* (.97) and to visual stimulation* (.92), writing sentences to dictation (.96), writing letters to dictation (.95), multiplication (.91), recognizing letters named in random order (.90), writing a paragraph (.89), following directions (.87), solving simple stated problems* (.86), and oral spelling (.85).

Performance by diagnostic groups is summarized in the tabulation. It is readily apparent that written spelling discriminates effectively between the simple aphasia and visual groups, both of which present a relatively mild reduction of language.

PERFORMANCE ON WRITTEN SPELLING

Diagnostic Group	Number	Mean	Percentage of Subjects Making Errors
Simple	12	0.50	33
Visual	8	5.38	75
Persisting Dysfluency [a]	7	*1.00*	*71*
Scattered findings	26	5.81	88
Sensorimotor	11	8.00	91
Auditory (1)	6	8.00	100
Auditory (2) [a]	17	*9.41*	*100*
Irreversible	12	9.92	100
Total aphasic subjects	75	6.08 (SD = 4.09)	81
Total nonaphasic subjects	50	0.76 (SD = 1.56)	36

[a] Not included in the totals.

Test 7. Oral Spelling

The correlation between written and oral spelling was .85, leaving about 28 per cent of the variance to be accounted for by factors not common to the two tests. Written spelling had a factor loading of .75 on visual discrimination, recognition, and recall and of .54 on language; while the third highest loading was .25, on visuospatial behavior. Oral spelling on the other hand had a loading of .84 on language and of 0.40 on visual discrimination, recognition, and recall; while the third highest loading, .28, was on gross movements of the speech musculature.

Correlations of .85 or above were obtained between oral spelling and repeating digits (.97), naming the days of the week (.94), repeating sentences (.93), counting to 20 (.93), expressing ideas (.93), writing a paragraph (.92), defining words (.91), writing sentences to dictation (.90), answering simple questions (.89), naming pictures (.89), repeating monosyllables (.88), completing sentences (.88), giving biographical information (.88), producing written sentences (.88), describing a picture (.87), and written spelling (.85). These correlations suggest that oral spelling is largely dependent upon ability to recall names of letters and learned letter sequences. A relationship with retention span is indicated by the high correlation with repetition of digits.

Most aphasic subjects tended to have a little more difficulty spelling words aloud than writing the same words to dictation. The most reasonable explanation appears to be that most aphasic subjects had a language deficit without involvement of visual processes and utilized visual information in writing. They were penalized more by oral spelling, which had a higher language and a lower visual component than written spelling.

Performance by diagnostic groups is summarized in the tabulation. Differences between means on oral and written spelling were negligible for all groups. Nonetheless individual patients were found

PERFORMANCE ON ORAL SPELLING

Diagnostic Group	Number	Mean	Percentage of Subjects Making Errors
Simple	12	0.67	25
Visual	8	5.63	75
Persisting Dysfluency [a]	7	1.00	71
Scattered findings	26	5.73	88
Sensorimotor	11	9.00	100
Auditory (1)	6	8.33	100
Auditory (2) [a]	17	9.94	100
Irreversible	12	10.00	100
Total aphasic subjects	75	6.28 (SD = 4.19)	81
Total nonaphasic subjects	50	0.62 (SD = 1.46)	26

[a] Not included in the totals.

87

who reversed the group trend by making more errors on written than oral spelling, frequently spelling words aloud correctly but writing them incorrectly, and usually confusing letters that look alike, such as *a* and *o, m* and *n, j* and *y, f* and *b,* or *u* and *w* in script. However, since the same subjects made aphasic as well as visual errors, qualitative analysis of writing errors is essential.

Test 8. Producing Written Sentences

Eighty-nine per cent of aphasic and 34 per cent of nonaphasic subjects made errors in writing sentences using given words, with means of 4.53 and 0.52 respectively. Writing sentences had a factor loading of .66 on language and .64 on visual discrimination, recognition, and recall.

Correlations above .85 were obtained with written spelling (.98), writing sentences to dictation (.96), writing a paragraph (.96), recognizing letters named in random order (.90), defining words (.90), writing letters dictated in random order (.90), repeating digits (.88), reading comprehension, paragraph (.88), oral spelling (.88), naming the days of the week (.87), solving simple stated problems* (.87), and following directions (.86).

These correlations seem to indicate that to produce written sentences one must have adequate vocabulary and adequate verbal re-

PERFORMANCE ON PRODUCING WRITTEN SENTENCES

Diagnostic Group	Number	Mean	Percentage of Subjects Making Errors
Simple	12	1.58	50
Visual	8	3.50	100
Persisting Dysfluency [a]	*7*	*0.71*	*29*
Scattered findings	26	4.85	96
Sensorimotor	11	5.73	100
Auditory (1)	6	5.50	100
Auditory (2) [a]	*17*	*5.88*	*100*
Irreversible	12	5.92	100
Total aphasic subjects	75	4.53 (SD = 5.01)	89
Total nonaphasic subjects	50	0.52 (SD = 0.93)	34

[a] Not included in the totals.

tention span to process verbal messages, as well as an acquired system of visual symbols.

Performance by diagnostic categories is summarized in the tabulation.

Test 9. Writing Sentences to Dictation

Ninety-six per cent of aphasic and 38 per cent of nonaphasic subjects made errors in writing sentences to dictation, with means of 5.43 and 0.80 respectively. Writing sentences to dictation had a factor loading of .68 on visual discrimination, recognition, and recall, and of .64 on language. For the aphasic population, errors generally increased as sentences increased in length.

Correlations of .85 or above were obtained with producing written sentences (.96), written spelling (.96), writing letters to dictation (.94), writing a paragraph (.93), writing words to auditory* (.93) and to visual stimulation* (.90), oral spelling (.90), recognizing letters named in random order (.88), repeating digits (.87), reading comprehension, paragraph (.86), matching printed to spoken words (.85), and naming the days of the week (.85).

Performance by diagnostic groups is summarized in the tabulation.

PERFORMANCE ON WRITING SENTENCES TO DICTATION

Diagnostic Group	Number	Mean	Percentage of Subjects Making Errors
Simple	12	2.17	83
Visual	8	4.50	88
Persisting Dysfluency [a]	7	0.27	86
Scattered findings	26	5.69	100
Sensorimotor	11	6.55	100
Auditory (1)	6	7.00	100
Auditory (2) [a]	17	6.94	100
Irreversible	12	7.00	100
Total aphasic subjects	75	5.43 (SD = 2.29)	96
Total nonaphasic subjects	50	0.80 (SD = 0.64)	38

[a] Not included in the totals.

Differential Diagnosis of Aphasia

Test 10. Writing a Paragraph

Ninety-five per cent of aphasic and 14 per cent of nonaphasic subjects made errors in writing a paragraph describing a picture. Mean errors were 4.64 (SD = 1.95) and 0.26 (SD = 0.72) respectively. The highest factor loadings for writing a paragraph were .69 on language and .58 on visual discrimination, recognition, and recall.

Correlations above .85 were obtained with producing written sentences (.96), writing sentences to dictation (.93), oral spelling (.92), written spelling (.89), repeating digits (.87), defining words (.86), naming the days of the week (.86), expressing ideas (.85), and completing sentences (.85).

Performance by diagnostic groups is summarized in the tabulation. Although scoring standards were not rigorous, in general only simple aphasia subjects and an occasional subject in the scattered-findings group were able to write an acceptable paragraph. Only seven out of 50 nonaphasic subjects made errors. In general subjects over 50 years of age performed as well as subjects under 50, and quality was consistent with educational level.

PERFORMANCE ON WRITING A PARAGRAPH

Diagnostic Group	Number	Mean	Percentage of Subjects Making Errors
Simple	12	1.33	67
Visual	8	4.38	100
Persisting Dysfluency [a]	7	1.57	43
Scattered findings	26	4.88	100
Sensorimotor	11	5.82	100
Auditory (1)	6	5.67	100
Auditory (2) [a]	17	6.00	100
Irreversible	12	6.00	100
Total aphasic subjects	75	4.64 (SD = 1.95)	95
Total nonaphasic subjects	50	0.26 (SD = 0.72)	14

[a] Not included in the totals.

DIAGNOSIS OF WRITING DISABILITIES

Most writing errors of aphasic subjects stemmed from language limitations. A subgroup of aphasic patients showed additional im-

90

pairment associated with impaired visual discrimination and impaired recall of learned visual symbols. A second subgroup showed severe impairment characterized by impaired visuospatial perception. Factor analysis of tests in Section D showed that all tests had their principal loadings on language; visual discrimination, recognition, and recall; visuospatial perception; or a combination of some of these factors [10]. Some tests had a higher loading on one factor and some on another, which is desirable for differential diagnosis of writing disabilities. (See Table 10.)

Table 10. Varimax Loadings of Visuomotor and Writing
Tests on Factors 1, 2, and 3

Test	Factor 1 (Language)	Factor 2 (Visual Discrimination, Recognition, Recall)	Factor 3 (Visuospatial Perception)
1. Copying Greek letters .... .15		.16	.89
2. Writing numbers to 20 .... .33		.53	.46
3. Reproducing wheel .... .15		.28	.70
4. Reproducing letters .... .31		.32	.71
5. Writing letters to dictation.... .49		.73	.31
6. Written spelling .... .54		.75	.25
7. Oral spelling .... .84		.40	.08
8. Producing written sentences .. .66		.64	.32
9. Writing sentences to dictation... .64		.68	.29
10. Writing a paragraph .... .69		.58	.24

Paralysis of the preferred hand is not a sufficiently disabling condition to preclude performance on any of the tests in this section, although the examiner should allow for initial awkwardness on first attempts to write with an untrained hand. It is a good thing for the examiner to try writing a paragraph with his own non-preferred hand, in order to be able to evaluate more realistically the performance of patients whose preferred hand is paralyzed. Occasional distortions of letters result from slips of the pencil, and sometimes reversals occur, since some individuals can produce mirror writing as easily as conventional writing with the non-preferred hand. However, these initial and comparatively minor difficulties do not resemble the consistent and persisting confusions of patients who have difficulty recalling visual forms of letters. If the examiner feels any doubt on this point he should defer judgment until the patient has adjusted to using the untrained hand and the initial clumsiness has been overcome. This usually occurs with a few days of systematic practice. Errors are not so readily reduced when visual recall is defective, and the same errors tend to be repeated again and again. The evidence is usually clear-cut and unmistakable if the patient is neurologically stable when examined. The best clinical rule is not to make a diagnosis of specific visual involvement when there is room for reasonable doubt. It is better to leave the question open until it can be resolved by further observation.

6

Disturbances of Numerical Relations and Arithmetic Processes

SUPPLEMENTARY TESTS

Level of competence in arithmetic can only be significant in comparison with previous learning and use. When it is important to estimate residual ability in relation to occupational needs, the Jastak and Bijou *Wide Range Achievement Test* is usually adequate, since items range in difficulty from kindergarten to college level.

TESTS INCLUDED IN SECTION E OF THE MINNESOTA TEST

In order to avoid unnecessary overlap with educational level, tests in Section E (Disturbances of Numerical Relations and Arithmetic Processes) are confined to functional skills related to the value of coins, setting a clock, and simple computations in addition, subtraction, multiplication, and division. Problems are similar to those usually included in third- and fourth-grade texts in most graded series, except for one problem in long division, which is usually introduced in fifth-grade textbooks. The performance of aphasic and nonaphasic subjects is summarized in Table 11.

It was observed very early that aphasic patients who improved in language also showed improvement of arithmetic skills on retest, even when no work on arithmetic had been done. Another early ob-

Differential Diagnosis of Aphasia

Table 11. Impairment of Numerical Relations and Arithmetic Processes:
Means, Standard Deviations, Median Scores, and Percentages
of Subjects Making Errors

Test	No.	Mean	SD	Median	Percentage of Subjects Making Errors
1. Making change					
Aphasics	75	0.79	1.72	0	35
Nonaphasics	50	0.00	0.00	0	0
2. Setting clock					
Aphasics	75	0.88	1.36	0	40
Nonaphasics	50	0.02	0.14	0	2
3. Simple numerical combinations					
Aphasics	75	3.01	3.49	2	69
Nonaphasics	50	0.12	0.44	0	8
4. Written problems: Addition					
Aphasics	75	1.12	0.88	1	68
Nonaphasics	50	0.20	0.45	0	18
Subtraction					
Aphasics	75	1.17	0.88	1	69
Nonaphasics	50	0.10	0.30	0	10
Multiplication					
Aphasics	75	1.49	0.75	2	85
Nonaphasics	50	0.58	0.64	0	50
Division					
Aphasics	75	1.57	0.76	2	84
Nonaphasics	50	0.56	0.81	0	36

servation was that patients who tended to reverse, distort, or omit letters on writing tasks tended to reverse, distort, or omit numbers also. In addition, patients who showed impairment of spatial perception on matching, drawing, copying, and object assembly tests usually had difficulty knowing where to put numbers down on the page when working problems. When multiplying by a number with two or three digits, for example, they often multiplied correctly, but recorded partial results in such a scattered fashion that it was impossible to add them.

Repeated observations such as these led to the conclusion that the arithmetic performance of aphasic subjects reflects the same kind of impairment observed on language tests. In fact most stated problems were deleted from early test forms because of the high correlation with language tests.

Factor analysis supported this hypothesis. No numerical or arithmetic factor appeared. All tests in this section had their highest factor loadings on language; visual discrimination, recognition, and recall; visuospatial behavior; or some combination of these three factors [10].

Aphasic subjects who could count or write numerals to 20 sometimes could not point to numbers named in random order, or write numbers dictated in random order; this was also true of letters of the alphabet. Numbers were usually relearned more readily than letters, perhaps because there are only 10 numerical symbols while there are 26 letters, and because names of numbers are usually easier to discriminate by ear than names of letters. Some aphasic patients had initial difficulty discriminating between numbers like 15 and 50, or 16 and 60, but this was usually readily resolved.

Patients with severe aphasia sometimes confused names of numbers more extensively. Most simple aphasia patients made errors in arithmetic because they could not remember learned combinations. A patient with mild aphasia might be able to tell himself that 2 times 2 is 4, but be less sure of 7 times 8. Patients who could not recall the multiplication tables sometimes circumvented the difficulty by adding seven 8's, for example, and occasionally although not always achieved correct results.

Patients with impaired visual discrimination tended to confuse 6's and 9's, 3's and 8's, and sometimes to reverse other numerals. Patients with spatial disorientation, in addition to reversing and distorting numbers and having difficulty in dealing with numerical arrays, frequently did not know how to read or write numbers composed of three or four digits, or combinations of dollars and cents. Some, however, were able to relearn the significance of positions in relation to the decimal point.

The spatial component of numerical and arithmetic tests is undoubtedly the reason that many left hemiplegics who are not aphasic have trouble with arithmetic.

Upon completion of this section of the test the examiner should

Differential Diagnosis of Aphasia

be able to determine if disruption of numerical and arithmetic processes stems chiefly from reduction of language, or if it is complicated by additional impairment of visual discrimination, recognition, and recall, by impairment of spatial perception, or by both of these factors.

Test 1. Making Change

All except three aphasic patients passed some items on Test 1. Although actual coins were used and instructions could be demonstrated by gesture, Test 1 had its highest factor loading, .56, on language, followed by loadings of .45 on visuospatial behavior, and .39 on visual discrimination, recognition, and recall. It is a little hard to explain the relatively large visuospatial factor on Test 1, although it may be that the discrimination of relative size involved in recognizing coins requires spatial information. One is also tempted to wonder if counting on fingers plays some role in the performance of aphasic patients, and if reduced sensory information interferes with such compensatory behavior. The origin of the word *digit* suggests some such hypothesis. On the other hand, abstract spatial dimensions undoubtedly play a role in higher mathematics, so the question becomes an abstruse one.

The highest correlations were obtained between making change and long division (.90), matching pictures* (.89), recognizing let-

PERFORMANCE ON MAKING CHANGE

Diagnostic Group	Number	Mean	Percentage of Subjects Making Errors
Simple	12	0.08	8
Visual	11	0.13	13
Persisting Dysfluency [a]	7	*0.14*	*14*
Scattered findings	26	0.35	31
Sensorimotor	8	0.36	27
Auditory (1)	6	1.50	83
Auditory (2) [a]	17	*1.47*	*43*
Irreversible	12	2.92	67
Total aphasic subjects	75	0.79 (SD = 1.72)	35
Total nonaphasic subjects	50	0.00	0

[a] Not included in the totals.

96

ters named in random order (.83), identifying items named serially (.80), matching printed to spoken words (.79), naming pictures (.79), following directions (.78), defining words (.78), writing sentences to dictation (.78), matching words to pictures (.77), reading comprehension, sentences (.77), writing a paragraph (.77), recognizing common objects named by the examiner (.77), giving biographical information (.77), and producing written sentences (.77).

Thirty-five per cent of aphasic and no nonaphasic patients made errors on Test 1. Performance by diagnostic groups is summarized in the tabulation.

The test is particularly useful for demonstrating retained abilities in subjects with severe aphasia, and for enabling the examiner to observe the breakdown of performance, which usually occurs when instructions become too long and too verbal.

Test 2. Setting Clock

Aphasic subjects tended to be able to set the hands of a clock to show when they got up, went to bed, and ate supper, but not to times designated by numbers. Setting the hands of a clock had a loading of .57 on visual discrimination, recognition, and recall; of .52 on language; and of .37 on visuospatial behavior. The relatively low load-

PERFORMANCE ON SETTING CLOCK

Diagnostic Group	Number	Mean	Percentage of Subjects Making Errors
Simple	12	0.00	0
Visual	8	0.50	38
Persisting Dysfluency [a]	7	*0.00*	*0*
Scattered findings	26	0.73	31
Sensorimotor	11	0.73	45
Auditory (1)	6	1.35	67
Auditory (2) [a]	17	*1.24*	*59*
Irreversible	12	2.25	83
Total aphasic subjects	75	0.88 (SD = 1.36)	40
Total nonaphasic subjects	50	0.02 (SD = 0.14)	2

[a] Not included in the totals.

97

ing on visuospatial behavior obtained in spite of the fact that on this test subjects were required to manipulate the movable hands of a clock to specific positions and relationships in space. Part of the explanation may simply be that the visuospatial factor is lower because reduction of language or of visual discrimination is more common in aphasic populations than impairment of spatial perception.

The highest correlations were obtained with matching pictures* (.88), following directions (.84), writing letters to dictation (.84), identifying items named serially (.83), solving simple stated problems* (.82), written spelling (.82), writing sentences to dictation (.81), producing written sentences (.79), counting to 20 (.78), writing a paragraph (.77), simple numerical combinations (.76), and recognizing letters named in random order (.76).

Forty per cent of aphasic subjects made errors in setting a clock, while one out of 50 nonaphasic subjects made one error. Performance by diagnostic groups is summarized in the tabulation.

Test 3. Simple Numerical Combinations

On Test 3 subjects are not required to produce answers, but merely to choose the correct number from a given array, which is presented visually and read to the subject as well. Test 3 had a factor loading of .57 on visual discrimination, recognition, and recall; of .52 on language; and of .37 on visuospatial behavior.

The highest correlations were obtained with long division (.90), addition (.87), subtraction (.80), producing written sentences (.80), writing letters dictated in random order (.78), reading comprehension, sentences (.77), identifying items named serially (.76), repeating sentences (.76), reading comprehension, paragraph (.76), writing sentences to dictation (.76), writing a paragraph (.76), setting a clock (.76), and solving simple stated problems* (.76).

Performance of subjects by diagnostic groups is summarized in the tabulation. In general, simple aphasia subjects gave the best performance on most of the numerical and arithmetic tests. Visual patients performed next best because they also presented comparatively mild aphasia. They did not do as well as simple aphasics,

98

however, because of the added complication of visual involvement. Sensorimotor patients, with severe reduction of language but no visual or spatial involvement, performed better on arithmetic than on language tests. They approached the performance of patients with scattered findings, who had more language but who showed scattered visual and spatial impairment. Irreversible patients showed consistently low performance. The performance of subjects with partial auditory imperception was much like that of irreversible patients, on initial testing at least, reflecting their inability to grasp instructions and retrieve names of numbers or learned combinations.

PERFORMANCE ON SIMPLE NUMERICAL COMBINATIONS

Diagnostic Group	Number	Mean	Percentage of Subjects Making Errors
Simple	12	0.25	25
Visual	11	1.75	50
Persisting Dysfluency [a]	*7*	*0.29*	*29*
Scattered findings	26	2.85	62
Sensorimotor	8	2.45	100
Auditory (1)	6	5.50	100
Auditory (2) [a]	*17*	*4.47*	*88*
Irreversible	12	6.25	100
Total aphasic subjects	75	3.01 (SD = 3.49)	69
Total nonaphasic subjects..	50	0.12 (SD = 0.44)	8

[a] Not included in the totals.

Test 4. Written Problems

After a good deal of experimentation it was decided to include one easy and one harder problem in addition, subtraction, multiplication, and division in this test. The easier problems involve carrying or borrowing numbers and some of the less common arithmetic combinations. The difference between the easier and harder items is that the latter involve longer series of computations and larger arrays of numbers, which present more opportunity for error to all subjects. If only computational errors appear, the difference is of no particular significance. Patients with visuospatial involvement, however, are frequently able to solve the simpler problems, but become confused when required to deal with more figures. Thus on this test kinds of errors are significant.

For the purpose of analysis the problems in addition, subtraction, multiplication, and division are treated as four separate tests. Findings will therefore be discussed separately, in the interests of differential diagnosis, since factorial structures presented some differences.

Addition. The highest factor loadings for addition were .63 on visual discrimination, recognition, and recall; .44 on spatial perception; and .27 on language.

The highest obtained correlations were with simple numerical combinations (.87), subtraction (.86), matching pictures* (.80), producing written sentences (.78), reading comprehension, paragraph (.76), solving simple stated problems* (.75), assembling the Wechsler manikin (.75), reading comprehension, sentences (.74), writing letters dictated in random order (.74), and writing sentences to dictation (.73).

Subtraction. Subtraction had a factor loading of .68 on visual discrimination, recognition, and recall; of .33 on language; and of .28 on visuospatial behavior. The highest correlations were obtained with addition (.86), simple numerical combinations (.80), matching pictures* (.79), reading comprehension, paragraph (.78), writing a paragraph (.76), solving simple stated problems* (.76), producing written sentences (.75), long division (.75), assembling Wechsler head (.73), written spelling (.73), oral reading (.72), writing letters to dictation (.71), and drawing a man (.71).

Multiplication. Multiplication had a factor loading of .39 on language; .38 on visual discrimination, recognition, and recall; and .34 on visuospatial behavior.

Correlations above .70 were obtained with written spelling (.91), recognizing common objects named by the examiner (.86), reproducing letters (.74), recognizing letters named in random order (.72), reading rate (.71), defining words (.71), and producing written sentences (.71).

The fact that multiplication had a higher factor loading on language than addition or subtraction probably stems from the fact that

Disturbances of Numerical Relations

MEAN ERRORS ON WRITTEN PROBLEMS

Diagnostic Group	Mean Errors
Simple	1.58
Visual	3.88
Persisting Dysfluency [a]	*2.71*
Scattered findings	5.50
Sensorimotor	6.45
Auditory (1)	7.16
Auditory (2) [a]	*7.00*
Irreversible	7.83
Total aphasic subjects	5.36
Total nonaphasic subjects	1.44

[a] Not included in the totals.

multiplication involves more learned combinations and a longer sequence of steps.

Nonaphasic subjects over 50 averaged more errors than subjects under 50, perhaps because of lower educational level, poor vision, and less recent use of arithmetic.

Division. Factor loadings on division were .45 on visuospatial behavior; .44 on visual discrimination, recognition, and recall; and .43 on language.

The highest obtained correlations were with solving simple stated problems* (.92), simple numerical combinations (.90), making change (.90), assembling the Wechsler manikin (.87), matching words to pictures (.87), jaw movements (.85), writing a paragraph (.81), producing written sentences (.80), tongue movements (.80), matching forms (.77), reading comprehension, paragraph (.76), and oral spelling (.76).

All arithmetic processes. Mean errors in each diagnostic category over the eight problems may be of some interest in describing the over-all performance of both aphasic and nonaphasic subjects. They are shown in the tabulation. The average time required to solve the eight problems was 6.56 minutes for nonaphasic subjects. There was no significant difference between the time required for subjects under 50 and subjects over 50. Only 30 out of 70 aphasic subjects for whom time was recorded completed all eight problems. The average time required for these 30 subjects was 10.83 minutes.

7

The Philosophy behind the Test

The Minnesota Test for Differential Diagnosis of Aphasia was not published for many years because it seemed desirable to keep the form flexible enough to allow continuous revision in the light of new observations. The biologist John Zachary Young has expressed a similar predilection in his book entitled *A Model of the Brain* [13]. Young wrote: "In our own work we have all the time been feeling our way by 'empirical' or 'intuitive' guesses as to what questions to ask the octopus. Indeed we have found that the nature of the problem has only appeared as we proceeded." It is always of crucial importance to learn to ask better questions and often a good many questions have to be asked before the nature of a problem is clear. The choice of questions is particularly relevant to test development, since a test is essentially a method of asking questions that lead the examiner to make observations upon which reasonable decisions and reliable predictions can be based.

Because it is important that observations be reproducible, *The Minnesota Test for Differential Diagnosis of Aphasia* was made available for experimental use in 1955. The test is published now, not only because of continued requests for copies and for permission to reproduce and to translate it into other languages, but because enough data have been analyzed to establish the usefulness of the test as a diagnostic tool, and to indicate that the information it yields is meaningful and consistent.

Since the published test is a revision of earlier forms, new tests and revised tests have been administered to different groups of subjects drawn from the same general hospital population. As a result over-all test data, such as error distributions over test sections, correlations between test sections, and comparison of test-retest results, have not been compiled. These data have been published for Form 6 [4], and are remarkably consistent. In a sense these data are of limited importance, since the critical dimensions, as previously pointed out, are the kinds of deficits revealed on various tests, and the over-all pattern of aphasic impairment that emerges. Clear definition of error types and error patterns gives us a starting point from which to think about the nature of aphasic disabilities.

This is not to say that quantification of data obtained from aphasic populations is not necessary. Observations must be repeated. It must be known what a test is measuring, insofar as this can be known, and the validity and internal consistency of a test must be established. Identification of significant trends or patterns of behavior is not possible without analysis of data. We must have numbers, as well as information about what the numbers represent, if we are to find even partial answers to the questions we know how to ask, and if we are to learn to ask more searching questions. Clinical impressions can be misleading, although they may generate "good 'intuitive' guesses" as to what questions to ask. The questions must be formulated, however, and appropriate observations must be made, recorded, and analyzed critically before answers can emerge.

To extend present knowledge of aphasia it is necessary to probe deeper into the kinds of perceptual and sensorimotor deficits, the dysarthrias, the disturbances of memory and retrieval, the disruptions of language, and the interferences with learning that brain damage produces, and to explore the interrelationships between these variables, and their effects upon communicative behavior.

This probing will require the continued development of new tests, new experiments, and new instruments. Young [13] has suggested that little is known about what properties of the world are encoded

Differential Diagnosis of Aphasia

by the nervous system. Almost nothing is known about how the nervous system stores or retrieves information, or about how neural processes work to effect feedback control. These are all formidable problems, but studying the effects of brain damage upon discrete behaviors is one method of increasing our understanding of what the brain does, and of the mechanisms it employs.

If it is a long time before the complex problems of aphasia are clearly understood, we can at least be confident that careful differential diagnosis is the *sine qua non* of all responsible clinical procedures in dealing with brain-injured patients. If the Minnesota Test helps the clinician to gain some insights into the nature of the difficulties aphasic patients experience, publication has been justified.

REFERENCES
AND SUPPLEMENTARY TESTS

References

1. Bricker, Amy, Hildred Schuell, and J. J. Jenkins. Effect of word frequency and word length on aphasic spelling errors. *J. Sp. Hear. Research*, 7, 183–192, 1964.
2. Chomsky, N. *Syntactical Structures*. The Hague: Mouton, 1957.
3. Fraser, C., U. Bellugi, and R. Brown. Control of grammar in imitation, comprehension, and production. *J. Verb. Learn. Verb. Behav.*, 2, 121–135, 1963.
4. Jenkins, J. J., E. Jiménez-Pabón, R. E. Shaw, and J. W. Sefer. *Schuell's Aphasia in Adults*. New York: Harper and Row, forthcoming, 1973.
5. Penfield, W., and L. Roberts. *Speech and Brain Mechanisms*. Princeton, N.J.: Princeton University Press, 1959.
6. Schuell, Hildred. *The Minnesota Test for Differential Diagnosis of Aphasia; Administrative Manual;* and *Card Materials* (drawings by Lawrence Benson). Minneapolis: University of Minnesota Press, 1965.
7. Schuell, Hildred, and J. J. Jenkins. The nature of the language deficit in aphasia. *Psychol. Rev.*, 66, 45–67, 1959.
8. Schuell, Hildred, and J. J. Jenkins. Reduction of vocabulary in aphasia. *Brain*, 84, 243–261, 1961.
9. Schuell, Hildred, J. J. Jenkins, and Lydia Landis. Relationship between auditory comprehension and word frequency in aphasia. *J. Sp. Hear. Research*, 4, 30–36, 1961.
10. Schuell, Hildred, J. J. Jenkins, and J. B. Carroll. A factor analysis of the Minnesota Test for differential diagnosis of aphasia. *J. Sp. Hear. Research*, 5, 350–369, 1962.
11. Thorndike, E. L., and I. Lorge. *The Teacher's Word Book of 30,000 Words*. New York: Teachers College, Columbia University, 1944.
12. Weisenburg, T. H., and Katherine E. McBride. *Aphasia*. New York: Commonwealth Fund, 1935.
13. Young, J. Z. *A Model of the Brain*. New York: Oxford University Press, 1964.

Supplementary Tests

1. Ammons, R. B., and H. S. Ammons. *Full-Range Picture Vocabulary Test*. Psychological Test Specialists, Box 1441, Missoula, Montana 59801.
2. Atwell, C. R., and F. L. Wells. *Wide-Range Vocabulary Test*. Psychological Corporation, 304 E. 45th Street, New York, New York 10017.
3. Bender, Lauretta. *Bender Visual Motor Gestalt Test*. Psychological Corporation, 304 E. 45th Street, New York, New York 10017.
4. Benton, Arthur. *Benton Revised Visual Retention Test*. Psychological Corporation, 304 E. 45th Street, New York, New York 10017.
5. Gates, A. I. *Gates Reading Tests*, Word Recognition, Primary and Advanced Primary. Psychological Corporation, 304 E. 45th Street, New York, New York 10017.
6. Goodenough, Florence F. *Goodenough-Harris Drawing Test* (revision and restandardization of Goodenough draw-a-man test). Psychological Corporation, 304 E. 45th Street, New York, New York 10017.
7. Gray, W. S., and H. M. Robinson. *Gray Oral Reading Tests*. Psychological Corporation, 304 E. 45th Street, New York, New York 10017.
8. Greene, H. A., A. N. Jorgensen, and V. H. Kelley. *Iowa Silent Reading Tests*, Elementary and Advanced (Vocabulary, Sentence Comprehension, Paragraph Comprehension). Psychological Corporation, 304 E. 45th Street, New York, New York 10017.
9. Jastak, J., and S. Bijou. *Wide Range Achievement Test*. Psychological Corporation, 304 E. 45th Street, New York, New York 10017.
10. Terman, L. M., and Maude A. Merrill. *Revised Stanford-Binet Scales*, 1960. Psychological Corporation, 304 E. 45th Street, New York, New York 10017.
11. Wechsler, David. *Wechsler Adult Intelligence Scale*. Psychological Corporation, 304 E. 45th Street, New York, New York 10017.